Roy "Bronco" B[illegible]
Bethel Co[illegible]
St. Paul, Minn.

Compliments of Mr. Hosokawa, Sunday editor of Minneapolis Tribune
Journalism Class 1959

WORD POWER

Talk Your Way to Life Leadership

WORD POWER

Talk Your Way to Life Leadership

by VERNON HOWARD

Englewood Cliffs, N. J.

PRENTICE-HALL, INC., 1958

LIBRARY OF CONGRESS
CATALOG CARD NUMBER: 58-11760

PRINTED IN THE UNITED STATES OF AMERICA

96387

WHAT THIS BOOK WILL DO FOR YOU

"How few know their own good," says John Dryden.

. . . This book will reveal to you your own fortunes of good!

"Chiefly, the mold of a man's fortune is in his own hands," observes Francis Bacon.

. . . This book will supply you with practical ways and means for attaining your own fortunes of good!

"How forcible are right words!" declares Job.

. . . This book will show you how the mighty force of your mind and daily words will change your life and make it what you wish!

TABLE OF CONTENTS

CHAPTER PAGE

CHAPTER PAGE

WORD POWER

Talk Your Way to Life Leadership

DAILY DYNAMITE — YOUR WORD POWER

Chapter 1

EVERY WORD YOU SPEAK HAS POWER IN your life!

Your speech habits make you happy or sad, confident or timid, relaxed or tense.

Says Professor Harry Overstreet: "Attention to words and phrases has profound psychological significance. He who would influence human behavior can hardly do better than to proceed quite seriously and persistently to overhaul his verbal equipment." [1]

Rightly used, your word power can magnificently change your life for the better!

This book will show you how to do it!

When you know how to effectively use the daily dynamite of your speech you will—in a very real way—talk your way to success. Make no mistake—new speech patterns mean new life patterns. Positive words charge our actions with fresh strength, correct our emotional responses in the right direction for dynamic living, channel our whole lives toward rest and freedom. Our business affairs, our love and sex life, our friendships, all take on a new look. In short, we create a new personality.

[1] Harry A. Overstreet, *Influencing Human Behavior* (New York: W. W. Norton & Company, Inc., 1925).

NEW WORDS CAN MAKE A NEW PERSONALITY

Now everyone agrees that a new personality is bound to make profound changes in the circumstances of the person. Well, new words *do* make a new personality. Writes Dr. Floyd I. Ruch: "Language . . . plays a far greater part in our lives than most of us realize in helping us to get along with other people and in affecting our thought and behavior."[2]

A reporter once interviewed the president of a large firm that manufactures sporting goods.

"To what do you attribute your success?" came the usual question.

"To correct speaking," was the reply.

The reporter jotted down a few notes. "I suppose you mean that you took a course in public speaking or perhaps mastered all the rules for superior conversation?"

The executive chuckled. "I wouldn't know a course in public speaking if it walked up and shook my hand."

The baffled reporter shook his head. "I don't understand."

The president reached over and picked up a small dictionary from the far corner of his desk. A few typed words were pasted on the cover. He said, "Every day for the past ten years I've seen this little message gently looking me in the face. And I always look back in deep gratitude."

The reporter read the words aloud:

Ten thousand words are a lot of power,
Make them work for you each hour.

The executive smiled at the reporter's bewilderment. "Shakespeare might have done better with the poetry," he said, "but he couldn't beat the message. You see, I estimate that I speak about ten thousand words a day, every one of them a tiny atom of power that can help or hinder me according to its character."

The reporter returned the smile. "I'd better have some details, please."

[2] Floyd L. Ruch, *Psychology and Life*, 4th ed. (Chicago: Scott, Foresman and Company, 1953).

WORD-POWER TECHNIQUES THAT WILL CHANGE YOUR LIFE

The president's reply was a nutshell version of what you will read in the following pages. You will find simple, workable word-power techniques that will effect practical changes in your whole mode of living. When you personally apply them you will feel better, think better, act better, *be* better.

It has been correctly observed that we *are* what we *think* we are. "As he thinketh in his heart, so is he." (Proverbs 23:7) It is equally true that we are what we *say* we are, for as philosopher Publius wrote: "Speech is a mirror of the soul: as a man speaks, so is he."

You see, it is a powerful truth that when you speak peaceful words you generate a peaceful self, when you allow cheery phrases to leave your lips you allow cheery emotions to live in your heart.

ABSORB THESE WORDS ABOUT WORDS

The psychological magic of words was proclaimed by an ancient thinker: "Pleasant words are as an honeycomb, sweet to the soul, and health to the bones." (Proverbs 16:24)

And their intimate relationship to human happiness in this modern day is excellently expressed: "Speech is that through which we most constantly influence one another. From the words of a mother to her child to the words of one diplomat to another, speech is the maker of psychological universes."[3]

All our religious, philosophical, and psychological approaches toward the achievement of human happiness must take words into account. Faith in God, the positive outlook, emotional control, and every other method that promises an uplifted life must consider the daily speech habits of the seeker. We cannot have faith in God while speaking faithlessly, we cannot main-

[3] Harry A. Overstreet, *The Mature Mind* (New York: W. W. Norton & Company, Inc., 1949).

tain a positive outlook while grouching, we cannot achieve emotional control while practicing verbal vagrancy.

You can get a clearer insight of the enormous role your everyday speech plays in your affairs by reviewing the things that have happened to you in the last few days as a result of your particular choice of words.

Perhaps the simple reply of "yes" to an invitation meant a delightful evening with friends.

Perhaps the complaint of, "It's too much for me," was the start of anguish over a problem that might have been easily solved by starting it with, "In one way or another I'll tackle and lick this thing."

Perhaps the compliment of, "I appreciate you," drew you and a loved one closer together in understanding.

FROM NOW ON—YOU ARE MASTER OF YOUR WORDS!

You have probably been reading this book silently up to this point. It's time to break the silence. If you are in any place at all where you can conveniently speak aloud I'd like you to read the below-listed declarations aloud. (If you are in a public place, pretend that you are reading them aloud; at your first opportunity, do so.)

Read them slowly, forcefully, believingly, just as if your whole heart and mind were absolutely convinced of their truths.

"My words are **daily dynamite.**"
"My words are **easy energizers.**"
"My words are **helpful friends.**"
"My words are **confidence-builders.**"
"My words are the **new me.**"

Add other good points that you want your words to be to you. From this point on, *you are their absolute master.*

Well! This has been a truth for all of us all along. We just didn't know it! But now we *do.* And we're down to business.

THE POWER OF WORDS-IN-ACTION

A physician who was keenly interested in mastering the knack of word power tells us of a fun-filled experiment he made during the course of a single day. Starting from the moment he left his home in the morning and ending with his return in the evening he became an eager observer of his words-in-action. He studied facial expressions, physical movements and emotional responses to the words spoken by him to some of those whom he contacted. Being a zealous football fan, he made a game of it by expressing results in football language:

> "Good morning!" I sunnily greeted the girl at the medical building's snack counter. When she cheerfully smiled back I complimented myself with, "That was at least a ten-yard gain!"
>
> On the way down the hall I met an associate who had just written a sparkling article on psychosomatic medicine. "Good reading, that piece of yours," I told him, "I'm curling up with it after dinner."
>
> He grinned. "Don't be surprised if you find some of *your* notes in there. I heard you speak last week."
>
> As I continued down the hall I thought. "Very good. You get what you give. I'd call that a twenty-yard gain right through the center of the line."
>
> When I arrived at my office I saw with some dismay that my nurse was late, leaving three patients waiting in the hall. Twenty minutes and twenty mutterings later she arrived, completely out of breath.
>
> "That's the second time this week, Miss Gans," I curtly remarked.
>
> She was clearly distressed but retained enough poise to reply with a show of spirit: "Sorry, doctor, but *my* car has flat tires, too."

KIND WORDS MAKE KIND PEOPLE

> "Oh, oh," I thought to myself, "thrown for a loss on that one." I apologized for my curt remark and added with a smile, "I may have a couple of flats myself some day."

Later in the day a widower in his middle sixties entered my private office. Previous visits had convinced me his problem was primarily emotional. He was, to put it bluntly, a sour, embittered individual whose problem was apparent. Having been in retirement for several months he no longer felt wanted. His previously responsible position had given him the ingredients he needed for a happy, balanced life. But now they were gone and his great need was for new outlets for his valuable life.

"Taken up that hobby yet?" I lightly inquired.

He looked me boldly in the eye. "Doctor," he said, "how would *you* like to spend *your* days building bird-houses for neighborhood kids?"

I studied him carefully as a football quarterback might study the opposing squad and called my signal. "How about people hobbies?"

He frowned. "*People* hobbies?"

I felt I was breaking through. "Sure. *People* hobbies. Where you exchange yourself with friends and new acquaintances."

He shook his head. "If you mean *church*," he replied, chasing me backward, "I already go. And if you mean sitting around and talking about the exciting new postage stamps from Outer Mongolia I'm just not interested."

I told myself it was time for a long pass. "Look, I'm not trying to force you to take up anything you don't really want. I'm talking about the kind of things you might like to do but have never tried. *Everyone* likes to do *something*."

"That makes sense," he said with a shrug. "It's a funny thing but for years I've wanted to take up square dancing." He paused and added, "Does that sound funny for a man of my age?"

I waved my hand toward him. "It's funny only as long as you think it is. So change your thinking. Go ahead, give it a try."

"I'll do it!" he declared, and then laughed, "but I'll confine myself to very small squares!"

A week or so later he practically square-danced himself into my office. "Not only do I square-dance," he chuckled, "but I have the liveliest partner you ever saw . . . and she's three years older."

I gave myself a touchdown on that one.

When I got home that evening I told my wife, "You know, when you consciously watch the power that your words have over others it gives you a feeling of *awe*." I immodestly added, "I feel almost like a dictator."

"Just don't dictate around here," she advised with a meaningful smile, "or you're liable to have a revolution."

I charged a fumble against myself with that dictator remark. But at least I gained something from her reply—fifty yards of humility!

TO UPLIFT YOUR ACTIONS—UPLIFT YOUR WORDS!

Nothing is more self-evident: Words lead to actions (as the doctor discovered).

"May I take you to dinner?" requests the young man of the lady of his choice. Her acceptance leads to action that is very nice.

"You broke my scooter!" Bobby screams to his playmate. His fiery words may lead to action that is not so nice.

Some of our words lead to actions that are obvious, but others are veiled. Some are immediate, some are delayed; some are vital, others are trifling. Without half thinking you can recall how your own words have led to situations which you either welcomed or regretted.

Benjamin Lee Whorf writes: "People act about situations in ways which are like the ways they talk about them."[4]

It follows that *by changing our words we can change our physical and mental actions. If certain ways of speaking result in unhappy circumstances, we are certainly able to replace them with other ways of speaking that will result in advantageous circumstances. There is no other possible conclusion.*

At this point it may sound like an oversimplification, but we have many wonderful discoveries to make! Let's take our cue from Thoreau: "If one advances confidently in the direction of

[4] S. I. Hayakawa, ed., *Language, Meaning and Maturity* (New York: Harper and Brothers, 1954), selections from "Etc.: A Review of General Semantics."

his dreams, and endeavors to live the life which he has imagined, he will meet with a success unexpected in common hours."

By this time it is obvious that our use of word power is not merely a system for building a larger vocabulary or for absorbing every rule for carrying on an adept conversation. The English language contains more than a half-million words and it is impossible and unnecessary to know them all. But among this half-million there are tens of thousands that are just right for the peaceful reply, the authoritative but kindly command, the generous compliment. So it is never a matter of a large vocabulary but a matter of wisely using the words we already know. We have already used positive word power on thousands of occasions (perhaps without realizing it); our present goal is to look around for additional uses which will pile blessing upon blessing upon both speaker and hearer.

WHAT, EXACTLY, IS WORD POWER?

So if word power is not a matter of a profuse vocabulary, exactly what is it?

It is the *psychological*—or *spiritual*—force of words that we will master. We are concerned with what words *do* for us, what they *create in our personalities,* not what they sound like as they slip from our tongues.

If you feel that you have not drawn from life those things you want and need, you can magically magnetize yourself by practicing what I call the Power Poem technique. A Power Poem is a simple, dynamic way of filling your heart, mind, and tongue with ideas that correspond to your desires. It is based on the old but always practical law that *like attracts like.* You will like it!

POWER POEMS PAY!

To use this technique, take pencil and paper and write down all the power-packed words you know that have some relation with your goal. Now use this list to compose a simple rhyme.

Keep your Power Poem short for easy repetition; five or six words will do. Here are some examples:

"I rest in the best!"
"Things fine are mine!"
"I have grace in this place!"
"God's cheer is now here!"
"A smile is my style!"
"I see I am free!"
"I rejoice in my choice!"
"I've a wealth of health!"

Never mind any awkward poetic structure you may run into; Longfellow isn't looking! We can overlook the fact that the meter *jerks* just as long as we know it *works!* And it does!

When you have created your Power Poem (or have selected one of the examples that most suitably expresses your need) you are ready to magnetize yourself. Say it out loud as often as you can, repeatedly scribble it on a sheet of paper, print it in large letters and hang it where you will frequently see it. As you *express* yourself about your desired state you *impress* yourself with it. You *become* what you *say* you are. And as the impression gains strength in your inner being you will feel a wonderful uplifting of your capacities to make reality out of your desire.

Now this is not hokus-pokus or starry-eyed mysticism. It's the real thing. Here is more proof from Professor Overstreet: "Words and phrases, then, are far more than mere symbols about which we can be relatively indifferent. They are perhaps the most powerful instrumentalities we possess for effectively and permanently lodging ideas in the mind."[5]

We have all had the experience of repeatedly thinking or singing catchy phrases from a popular song. They run through our minds without conscious invitation, like mischievous little imps. And to some degree or other we take on the very nature of their insistent chorus—happy hummings elevate our spirits, mournful ones depress us. We are now borrowing this curious trait of the mind for constructive purposes.

[5] Overstreet, *Influencing Human Behavior.*

You see, once we deeply implant an idea it takes root and grows with very little further conscious effort on our part. Its efforts are automatic.

INVITE YOURSELF TO NEW VITALITY

Now since your world is certainly surrounded by an abundance of good things, why not implant only those positive ideas which blossom after their kind? Your invitation starts and finishes their pleasant work of revitalization.

A woman of thirty reported excellent results with the Power Poem procedure. Chained by doubts as to her ability to go out and find a suitable job, she selected the Power Poem, "I see I am free!"

"I frankly confess," she said, "that I not only doubted my job-finding ability but doubted my strength to stir up my inner ability with a Power Poem. But it was a case of sink or swim so I put everything I had—which wasn't much—into it. As I encouraged myself with the verse I also created mental visions of myself as comfortably and eagerly doing the work for which I was qualified. I told myself, 'I see I am free! . . . free to apply, free to speak confidently at the interview, free to accept a fair offer.'

"I placed freedom in my heart and my birth certificate in my hand, and walked up to the personnel office of a company that manufactured military supplies. To my surprise I heard myself saying 'no' to the job offer, for it involved unsuitable working hours. (My earlier visions had pictured me as eagerly jumping at the first chance!)

" 'Well,' I said to myself as I returned to my car, 'something's happening! I wonder how far I can carry this thing?' A glorious feeling of abandonment that I had not known since childhood coursed through me. I gratefully repeated my verse, secure in the knowledge that I was, to a great measure, free from self-doubt. I knew that with a little leg-work I could get the very position I wanted. And I *did!*"

Obviously, there was no mere "luck" involved in the woman's triumph. By recognizing her problem as one of feelings of inadequacy she overcame them through the scientific use of word power. Her successful technique backs up the statement of Wendell Johnson: "A technique is a way of doing something, and language may be viewed and evaluated as a technique for accomplishing personality adjustment."[6]

SAY IT—AND BE IT!

Here is the all-important precept that sums up the whole happy truth about word power:

Talk the way you'd like to be and you'll be the way you talk!

Read it again:

Talk the way you'd like to be and you'll be the way you talk!

Like to be courageous? Speak courageously! Like to be a leader? Speak with authority! Like to be more loving? Speak loving words! Loosen up and speak up!

You can easily prove this precept by noting that you *already* talk the way you are. For example, the man who frequently says "Thank you" to the mailman reveals a certain trait of courtesy; the motorist who frequently growls at the gas-station attendant for failing to clean the windshield reveals a certain trait of irritability.

An observing reader may remark at this point, "Ah, but haven't you got the cart before the horse? Shouldn't the motorist correct his inner irritability *first* so that he will then naturally speak courteously?"

I'm glad you brought this up. We discuss the matter of natural feeling later on in the book, but for now I'd like to say this:

Of course his inner irritability must be corrected. But where shall he start? What *tool* will he use for correction? *Speech!* As he hears himself speaking in a new way he will gradually gain a new insight into himself that will promote a *natural feeling* of courtesy. And this new *feeling* of courtesy in turn promotes the *actual act* of courtesy. Back and forth it goes, speaking to

[6] Wendell Johnson, *People in Quandaries* (New York: Harper and Brothers, Publishers, 1946).

feeling, feeling to speaking until they become one. He literally becomes a man of his word! This movement is described by Professor Gardner Murphy: "The world of symbols [words] comes from the world of action and returns constantly to the world of action." [7]

Always remember: *Whatever you say to others you also say to yourself.* Want to be kind to yourself? Speak kindly to others. Well! *The Golden Rule is a scientific principle!*

RESOLVE RIGHT NOW TO SPEAK ONLY IN A POSITIVE, CHEERFUL, CONFIDENT WAY

Get down to business right now by resolving to speak only in a positive, constructive, cheerful, confident manner (and don't forget, this always includes speaking to yourself!). Regardless of what happens or whom you meet, talk in a manner that represents your highest ideals. As often as possible, drop in optimistic and hopeful remarks.

Don't just wait for speech opportunities to come your way (for you will meet many folks who do not know the secret of word power and thus cannot "set you up" for the right words) but *go out of your way to create your own opportunities.* Remember, you are pioneering a new way of life for yourself, so you must march boldly forward. Think of each positive word as one step closer to the forest clearing where you will dwell in your new peace and security.

This should be easy to accomplish. You will develop an increasing naturalness, an ease, and more than that you will find an eagerness to go farther and faster. There are bright rewards ahead—and you are valiantly on your way!

HOW TO PLAY A DIFFERENT TUNE

Once upon a time there lived a band of little elves who dwelled in the Musical Forest. They were happy little elves who played gay little tunes all day long on their musical instru-

[7] Gardner Murphy, *Personality* (New York: Harper and Brothers, 1947).

ments. But there was one little elf named Dum-Dum-Dum who was not happy. He was unhappy because all he could play on his drum was *dum-dum-dum.* He was tired of playing only *dum-dum-dum.* Every other little elf could play such merry melodies as *bing-bing-bing* and *ping-ping-ping* and *zing-zing-zing.*

But poor Dum-Dum-Dum could only play *dum-dum-dum.* Which depressed him very much.

"Come, Dum-Dum-Dum!" the happy little elves called to him. "Come and play a happy *bing-bing-bing* with us!"

"How can I play *bing-bing-bing* when I can only play *dum-dum-dum?*" he gloomily asked.

"Never mind," the elves called back, "just come on over and help us play a cheerful *ping-ping-ping.*"

"But how can I turn my *dum-dum-dum* into *ping-ping-ping?*" he asked as he gloomily turned to leave.

"Come back!" they shouted. "Come back and join us in a lilting *zing-zing-zing!*"

"If I could only play *zing-zing-zing* instead of *dum-dum-dum,*" he sobbed as he fled into the deep forest. As he aimlessly wandered he could hear all the other happy little elves playing all their joyous little tunes.

YOU ARE **NOT** LIMITED!

"Oh, if I could just change my tune," he moaned as he droopily sat on a toadstool, "but I guess I am doomed to *dum-dum-dum* all my little life."

He wept-wept-wept in unison with his *dum-dum-dum.*

All of a sudden he looked up! *Tweet-tweet-tweet!* he heard the gay lilt of an approaching piccolo.

"Tweet-tweet-tweet!" said a pretty little girl elf named Tweet-Tweet-Tweet as she poked her sunny smile through the bushes. "Hurry, Dum-Dum-Dum!" she called, "we are about to play another happy song!"

Now Dum-Dum-Dum knew a pretty little girl elf when he saw one. He quickly brushed away his tears and replied, "Nice of you to ask me, but you know very well I am limited to my *dum-dum-dum.*"

"Don't be so dumb, Dum-Dum-Dum," exclaimed the girl elf as she wagged a reproving finger. "You know very well you can play anything you *want* to play."

The unhappy little elf quizzically tilted his head. "But how can that be so? I've been playing only *dum-dum-dum* all my life."

She tenderly patted his wet cheek with her handkerchief. "Poor little Dum-Dum-Dum," she sweetly sympathized, "someone ought to tell you the facts of life. Don't you know that you can play *tra-la-la* or *zing-zing-zing* or any other happy melody that you wish?"

His tears gushed forth once more as he desperately clutched her hand. "Do you think . . ." he sobbed, "do you *really* think there's hope?"

She laid a soft hand alongside his feverish cheek. "Remember," she whispered, "this is the Musical Forest where *anyone* can play *anything*. All you have to do is *do* it. Come," she beckoned, "I will show you."

So he shyly followed her back to where all the other happy elves were about to play another happy concert.

"Here!" exclaimed Tweet-Tweet-Tweet as she handed him a flute. "Play this. See what happens!"

"But surely it will come out the same old *dum-dum-dum,*" he miserably objected, "for that is the only tune I know."

TRY IT—AND BE HAPPILY SURPRISED!

"Try it!" cheered all the elves in chorus.

So he lifted the flute and to his surprise out came a cheerful little *tra-la-la.*

"See!" declared the girl elf, "already you are playing a different tune!" She handed him a trumpet and commanded, "Now try *this!*"

To his astonishment he heard himself playing a very tooty *toot-toot-toot.*

"There!" triumphantly exclaimed the little girl elf, "you are no longer just Dum-Dum-Dum of the *dum-dum-dum!* Now try *this,*" she said as she handed him a piano (for she was very strong for a girl elf).

As he touched the piano his fingers magically played a very tinkly *tinkle-tinkle-tinkle.*

"At last!" shouted Tweet-Tweet-Tweet, "at last you know you can change your tune!"

"Amazing!" cried Dum-Dum-Dum as he played *tra-la-la.* "And fantastic and astonishing!" he declared as he easily repeated *ping-ping-ping* and *zing-zing-zing.*

"Hooray for Dum-Dum-Dum!" cheered all the elves in chorus. "Hooray for our little friend who has found himself!"

"Hooray for me!" he modestly agreed.

So from that day forth little Dum-Dum-Dum was one of the happiest of all the happy little elves in the Musical Forest. All day long he went about playing his new merry melodies of *tra-la-la* and *tinkle-tinkle-tinkle* and *zing-zing-zing.*

Which made everyone love him very much.

DARE TO PLAY A DIFFERENT TUNE!

Are you dejected because you think that the only tune you can play is the dreary *dum-dum-dum* you have been playing all your life? If so, take a lesson from our little elf. Like him, you can learn to play any merry tune you choose. All you have to do is *do* it. You are not—I repeat, you are *not*—confined to mournful, monotonous music. The gay violins, the cheery flutes, the soothing harps are yours for the playing.

There is no life so filled with *dum-dum-dum* that it cannot be turned into a lilting *zing-zing-zing!* John K. Williams contributes: "The world moves forward in surges as here a man and there a woman makes a fresh and daring discovery, or proposes some bold new idea. If the truth were known, most of such contributions to progress probably come from the subconscious mind of some person who has broken the bounds of conventional, conscious thinking." [8]

[8] John K. Williams, *The Knack of Using Your Subconscious Mind* (Englewood Cliffs, N. J.: Prentice-Hall, Inc., 1952).

The thing we all need most is more *daring*. So *dare* to play a different tune. Consider every positive word as a single, lovely note in the sweeping symphony of your life.

You will be delightfully surprised at all the folks who will want to attend your concert!

REVIEW THESE DYNAMIC IDEAS

1. Your daily words are packed with dynamite!

2. Know that your powers of speech can wonderfully change your life.

3. Realize that word power is a simple, practical means for self-elevation.

4. Claim your mastery over the enormous forces of your words.

5. Talk the way you'd like to be and you'll be the way you talk!

6. Resolve to speak positively, cheerfully, confidently.

7. Think of each positive word as an upward step.

8. Step out, speak up, create your own opportunities for life-advancement through speech-strength.

9. Dare to play a different verbal tune—know that your life can be filled with gay melodies.

10. Get down to business right now!

WHAT WORD POWER WILL DO FOR YOU — RIGHT NOW

Chapter 2

WHILE PREPARING THE MANUSCRIPT for this book I chatted with dozens of folks, including friends, casual acquaintances, professional men, psychologists. Whenever the opportunity arose to bring up the subject of word-power I asked the question, "Supposing you determined to use the power of your words as levers for life-improvement? What's the first thing you would do?"

WHAT ADVANTAGES DOES WORD POWER OFFER?

When I asked this of an attorney he thoughtfully replied, "Well, now, I like to think of myself as a practical man. The first thing I would do is find out just what advantages it offers. I'd want to know if it was something I can practice while going about my daily schedule. I'd like to see just how practical it was for my personal use. Whenever I prepare a case for court I always try to figure out the rewards of this or that procedure; I'd do the same with word-power." He added, "Incidentally, the idea of deliberately using your daily speech for personality improvement sounds like an appealing adventure."

"All right," I said, "let's adventure. We've been discussing the topic for the last half-hour so tell me, what appealing advantages does it offer you?"

EASY-TO-USE TOOLS ARE ALWAYS ON HAND

He laughed. "Well, my *equipment* is always on hand."

"Your *equipment?*" I asked.

"My tongue," he chuckled.

"What else?" I urged.

YOU CAN PRACTICE ANYWHERE, ANYTIME

"Well, I can practice it anywhere, anytime . . . at home, the office, on top of the Eiffel Tower if I like."

"Any other advantages?"

He shrugged. "Since I'm always talking *anyway,* why not talk *creatively?*" He grinned. "My wife says I talk too much; maybe even that's an advantage."

"What else do you like about it?"

"You're asking leading questions," he replied, "but now that I think of it I'd need no textbooks, no set-aside periods, nothing out of the ordinary in the course of a day. As I said, it's anywhere, anytime."

I looked at my watch and saw it was time to leave. "I'll lead you again. Give me one more good idea."

IT'S EASY TO CHECK YOUR DAILY PROGRESS

"Well, it seems that if and when I make a blunder with my *lips* I can immediately catch myself with my *ears.*"

"In other words, it's a simple thing to check and chart your daily progress?"

"That's about it."

I rose and wagged a friendly finger at him. "I'll expect you to practice what you preach."

He walked with me to the door. "Before you go, turn and read that motto on my wall. I think it will answer your question."

The motto, taken from Boswell's *Life of Samuel Johnson,* read:

EVERYTHING THAT ENLARGES THE SPHERE OF HUMAN POWERS, THAT SHOWS MAN HE CAN DO WHAT HE THOUGHT HE COULD NOT DO, IS VALUABLE.

We now have a clear idea of the practical, everyday possibilities of our speech powers. We know we have a loaded machine-gun. Now to find the target.

KNOW WHAT YOU WANT FROM LIFE!

All gain starts with *desire.* John K. Williams neatly sums it up: "The foundation stone of any achievement is desire, that which is wanted intensely by the individual. This is the starting point. It is the infinite urge of life—any life—for expression and expansion." [1]

Before you *bought* that new home you *wanted* that new home, before you took that trip you desired to take it, before you decided on steak for dinner you wanted that steak.

So . . . *what do you want from life?*

Perhaps a sparkling personality.

Maybe deeper love experiences.

Would you like freedom from feelings of frustration?

Perhaps it's a richer religious life.

Everyone wants a calm, serene outlook.

What do you want from life?

When you set out to drive to the mountains you usually got there because you knew your desired destination. When you sit down to read a good book you gain your reward from that book because you knew what you wanted.

You are now reading this book because you want something. This is an excellent sign, for we all want something; it's a part of healthy human make-up. It proves you are reaching for better things. Which is every man's right.

[1] John K. Williams, *The Knack of Using Your Subconscious Mind* (Englewood Cliffs, N. J.: Prentice-Hall, Inc., 1952).

MAKE YOUR DESIRE SPECIFIC—THEN VERBALIZE IT

Now make your desire specific. Break it down. Know exactly what you want. No matter how impossible or improbable it seems at the moment, regardless of past puzzlements or disappointments, make your desire clear in your mind. This is all you need to do for the moment—but it is essential. Say out loud to yourself, "This is what I want, here is my goal." Now state exactly what it is.

It may sound elementary that you should deliberately verbalize your desire—you may believe you often do this anyway. But a deliberate, conscious, outspoken claim just now will do much to nudge you closer your goal. Here's a happy surprise: The minute you determinedly specify your goal is the same minute it starts to reveal itself as a distinct *possibility*—and you're on your way. (It's like the minute you decided on a vacation at the mountains—you *started* toward the mountains.)

So clearly desire and you'll clearly acquire. As long as it is reasonable and within the possibilities of human attainment, you will more and more believe in *it* and in *yourself* in relationship toward it. (And the only thing I will accept as an unreasonable goal for you is a pole-vault to the moon—all else is reasonable.)

"Dad," cried little Jimmy, "I want a bicycle."

"*Why* do you want it?" asked Dad.

"Just because I want it."

"That's no answer to my question."

"That's no question to my answer."

"You want it just because you want it?"

"Just because I want it."

"No explanations, no doubts, no questions?"

"None. I want it because I want it."

Dad thoughtfully nodded. "I can't think of a *better* reason. Let's go get that bicycle."

Here's the idea: You now know what you want and you know your desire is both possible and rewarding. Forget everything else except normal means of attainment. If you involve yourself with explanations or doubts or questions (or even failures) you lose your goal's sight—and it takes flight. Dr. Fritz Kunkel superbly sums up: "The principle is: be creative, at the risk of failure; and if you fail, do not give up; be creative again." [2]

ASK FOR WHAT YOU WANT—**CORRECTLY**

Picture yourself as a real estate agent who is showing a home to prospective buyers. As a good salesman you want very much to sell them the property. So you guide them about, pointing out all the desirable features, saying, "Notice the three large bedrooms . . . see the spacious back yard . . . here's a two-car garage . . . quiet neighborhood, isn't it?"

When you finish your inspection you are ready to ask for their signatures on the papers. But suppose that instead of doing this you step into your car and say, "I want to sell you this house but I don't believe I can. Nice seeing you. Good-by." And off you go.

What do you think? You think you'd better spin that car around and ask for what you want—their signatures.

Unfortunately, many of us forget one of the most important rules of life-salesmanship. That rule is simply—*ask for it!* When you know what you want—*ask for it.* Almost any good book that teaches successful salesmanship stresses this point, for what good is it to know what you want if you don't step boldly up and ask for it? The rule is just as applicable to life-salesmanship as it is to the real estate business.

YOU ASK FOR EVERYTHING YOU GET

The overwhelming influences and circumstances that are in your life right now are there because you asked for them—either correctly or incorrectly. In one way or another, we ask for almost everything we get. Benjamin Disraeli, England's great statesman, knew this when he declared: "Man is not the creature of circumstances. Circumstances are the creatures of men."

[2] Fritz Kunkel, *In Search of Maturity* (New York: Charles Scribner's Sons), p. 238.

Sound like strong talk?

Let's see.

Take such a common thing as the clothes you wear. They now please or displease you because you first asked for them. Or take your choice of television entertainment. You view quiz shows because you desire them, you ask for them.

How about your personality itself? You speak cheerfully or grumpily because you first *trained* (a form of asking) yourself to speak in these ways. You happily or gloomily react to an unexpected switch in plans because you first asked for and then implanted these reactions as part of your personality.

YOUR DAILY SPEECH INDICATES WHAT YOU ASK FROM LIFE

Our daily speech is a certain indicator of what we are asking from life. To illustrate this, let us look in on a little drama. Our cast includes a sincere, honest, hard-working man and his equally sincere wife. Outside of the obvious fact that the husband is a man and his wife a woman, there is just one other difference—one is a speech-slave and the other a speech-master.

> *Husband (dragging home after a tough day's work at the sweat-shop):* Am I washed out!
>
> *Wife (sympathetically):* Hard day, dear?
>
> *Husband (kicking off shoes): Awful* day . . . do you know what terrible thing happened?
>
> *Wife (handing him his slippers):* Tell me.
>
> *Husband (growling):* You know that Bob Gripsag? . . . that miserably bungling Gripsag? Had to plough through ten miles of screeching traffic just to fix up one of his usual blunders.
>
> *Wife (sweetly smiling):* Did it come out all right, dear?
>
> *Husband (scowling with self-satisfaction):* After I told him off it did! *(gleefully rubbing his hands)* Boy, did I tell him off!
>
> *Wife:* Did it help, dear?
>
> *Husband (triumphantly):* Well, it sure helped *me!* Get out the old steam I always say . . . makes you feel *better* . . . *(groaning, holding head)* Boy, do I feel *awful.*

Wife (setting table): Come, dear, your favorite dinner.

Husband (sitting down, frowning): Not much of an appetite tonight . . . *(scowling)* That blundering Gripsag . . . *(rising)* I'd better lie down.

Wife (putting a pillow under his head): There . . . that better?

Husband (sourly): I suppose *you* had a miserable day, too?

Wife (cheerfully): Oh, no, quite nice as a matter of fact. I did have to turn off the water long enough to fix that leaky faucet . . .

Husband (explosively interrupting): That *plumber!* . . . do you know what he charged us? . . .

Wife (tenderly): Take it easy, dear . . . all's well.

Husband (feebly turning over, muttering): Hope I can get some sleep tonight . . . *(growling)* That Gripsag . . . that plumber . . .

Wife (stroking his forehead): Go to sleep, darling . . .

Husband (fitfully snoring): Zzzz . . . zz . . . zzzz . . . zz.

Let's face it. The poor man asked for it. He talked himself into a nervous despair and missed his favorite dinner besides. His poor wife didn't ask for it, but like lots of poor (or rather, rich) wives she had to be the strong one. Let's hope she tells him about happiness-building through word power!

We draw those negative, destructive circumstances into our lives because we ask amiss. And we ask amiss because we know no other way to cope with our problems. We believe life is cheating us and so we strike back. But the wise Emerson points out, "It is as impossible for a man to be cheated by any one but himself, as for a thing to be, and not to be, at the same time."

BELIEVE THAT WHAT YOU ASK FOR WILL BE YOURS!

Cheat yourself no longer! Ask for it correctly—in faith. Now it is a profound truth that we almost always *do* ask in faith, but faith can be negative as well as positive. When the real estate agent drives away from his clients because he has faith he cannot sell the house he receives what he asks for—*nothing*. What is faith but simply what we actually believe in the very depths of our hearts and minds? When we practice negative faith we withdraw and complain, thus receiving exactly what we ask for —a withdrawn, complaining way of life.

YOU CAN CHOOSE THE WAY YOU SPEAK

It will help you to ask in the right way if we emphasize a point we lightly touched upon in Chapter 1 concerning your personal position with word power.

You can *choose* the way you speak!

You have freedom of speech. You can talk any way you like. There are no policemen lurking about the tip of your tongue.

Think of your freedom of speech as freedom of *reach*—you can verbally reach out in any direction you select.

Reflect a moment what this means.

It means that by a simple act of speech-switch you can switch your life toward those things for which you are asking.

As a California orange grower remarked, "If there's one thing in life over which I exert maximum control, it's the way I talk. Just as I choose the proper cultivation for my orchards I choose the correct cultivation of my speech. And believe me, I get good fruit in both my orchards and my life."

Do you see how a faithful choosing of correct speech habits should be as much a part of our lives as the very air we breathe? Do you see why St. James advised, "Ask in faith, nothing wavering."? (James 1:6)

Remember these two vital steps:

1. Know exactly what you want.
2. Ask for it correctly—in positive, constructive faith.

So take these steps now, nothing wavering, and in due time you will receive what you ask for. It's the law!

HOW ONE MAN DID IT

I'd like to pass on to you a fascinating story that sharply illustrates all the good ideas we have covered so far in this chapter. It's a perfect example of practical word-power-in-action for it tells of a man who knew what he wanted—and got it.

I once attended an authors' banquet where I found myself seated between two good friends, one a prominent television producer and the other a writer of documentary films. The TV producer told us a remarkable story of how he had combined word power with common sense in licking his problem of . . . well, let's call it immoderate eating habits.

"I am one of those men who has to watch his waistline every minute," he told us. "For years I tried diet, denial, and dessert-dodging with little or no success. I used will-power and pill-power until they seemed to possess kill-power. One day, after doing fairly well for two or three days, *bingo!* . . . my neighbors invited my wife Patty and me over for an outdoor barbecue. I looked enviously at my wife's trim figure and groaned, 'Lucky you, do you know what's going to happen to me over there?'

" 'Of course,' she said, 'and so do you. You'll get one sniff of those spareribs and collapse as if from hunger. And when you revive you'll eat just like a man who *really did* collapse from hunger.'

" 'Why?' I moaned, 'Why does this have to happen to *me?*'

IT NEED **NOT** HAPPEN TO YOU

"She shrugged. 'It doesn't have to, you know.'

" 'Easy for you to shrug,' I scowled, 'you and your high metabolism.'

"She held up a knowing finger. 'For five dollars I'll give you my secret formula.'

" 'Make it five cents,' I bargained, 'and you've got a deal.'

" 'Okay,' she said, somewhat more seriously, 'but I want you to follow my directions implicitly. One slip and I give you up.'

"I tried to mask my desperate curiosity by casually remarking, 'I'm waiting, doctor.'

" 'Here's what I want you to do. Go on over to the barbecue. Take some spareribs. If there's plenty of extras, take seconds. If no one's looking, take thirds.'

"I frowned. 'That's a funny reducing system . . . where'd you get it?—from the *Glutton's Handbook?*'

" 'I'm the doctor,' she reminded. 'I want you to simply dig in. Eat all you want.'

"My frown deepened. 'You know very well that's the very thing I *want* to do. I don't get it.'

" 'Here's the point,' she went on. 'Your life is based on *wants.* In this particular case you have two conflicting wants—you *want* to eat spareribs and you want *not* to eat spareribs. Right?'

" 'Right,' I agreed.

" 'Okay, so you must want *not* to eat spareribs more than you want *to* eat spareribs. Right?'

" 'Right again.'

UNDERSTAND **THIS**

" 'So it's simple. The thing you've got to do is to make the *not want* emotion stronger than the *want* emotion, for when you have two strong emotions the dominating one always wins. Your goal is to be dominated by the stronger emotion of *moderation.*'

" 'You've been reading psychology books,' I accused.

" 'And you've been *listening* to me,' she grinned. 'But let's get on. I want you to repeat to me what you first said when we got the invitation.'

" 'Something like, *I'm sunk!*' I said.

" 'And that's your big mistake,' she declared, sounding like a mother scolding a naughty child. 'You claimed failure before you even started; so it's no wonder you're sunk.'

" 'Now wait just a minute,' I interrupted, 'if you're claiming that I can keep myself in check just by *saying* I can you're reading the wrong books.'

" 'You want your measly nickel back?' she threatened.

" 'Keep talking,' I miserably sighed.

" 'All right. Now before we go over I want you to make a declaration of independence. I want you to say to yourself, and also out loud, something like, "I like spareribs and I'm going to have spareribs. I may even stuff myself like a starving hound-dog, but whatever happens . . ." she held up a finger for emphasis, "Whatever happens, I will not *fear spareribs.*" '

" 'Who's afraid of spareribs?' I laughed.

YOU ARE YOUR OWN MASTER!

" '*You* are afraid of spareribs,' she countered. 'They've got you bluffed. You think you can't resist them. You said you were sunk because you *believed* you were sunk. Now I want you to declare that you are bigger than spareribs anytime. You can take them or leave them. They have *no* domination over you. You are always their master.'

" '*Then* what happens?'

" 'Then you go on over and enjoy the most delicious spareribs you have tasted in years. And regardless of how many you take I want you to come right back here and declare your freedom all over again. I want you to tell yourself—in spite of all evidence to the contrary—that you are your own master. You *are* your own master.'

"I groaned. 'Just pass the spareribs and call me Bulgy.'

" 'You may or may not practice moderation at this particular barbecue,' she continued, 'but that is not at all important. The vital thing is to impress yourself with the truth that you need not be dominated by immoderation. As this idea increases in clarity and power your *dominating* want will be for *moderation*—and away fly the pounds.'

" 'If it works I'll buy you a new hat,' I told her.

"And three weeks later she got her hat!

"It *did* work. Slowly at first, but I was amazed at the power that my new insight gave me. For the first time in years I knew I was free from the domination of a false faith."

The producer ended his story with the remark, "I don't know if it will work for you fellows; maybe you don't have such a wise little wife. All I know is that it worked magnificently for me!"

His success is explained by psychology: "Words have almost

magic power to change the way we look at things and hence to change our ways of reacting to them emotionally."[3]

SPEAK AND THINK SUCCESS—NOT FAILURE

You see, when we no longer fear a thing—even a defenseless sparerib!—we gain emotional control over it. As long as the producer spoke and thought failure he induced that failure into his problem. And every time he failed he reinforced his conviction that future failures were his dismal lot in life. It is always according to our faith. This is not merely a religious precept, it is true in every personal endeavor.

"Face your problem," psychology advises, "and you lick it." We might twist it to, "Lick your sparerib—even bite it—and you face freedom."

The producer's story is not at all intended as the exact answer in every case, but it does suggest a psychologically-sound technique that you might well add to your other sound approaches or your doctor's counsel.

And though the above story illustrates a particular problem, you might well apply it to the particulars of your own desires. Therefore, it will be helpful to take a step-by-step review of the producer's plan, while keeping in mind your personal goals.

MAKE THESE PERSONAL APPLICATIONS

1. Banish all your previous speech and thought habits concerning your problem. (They failed you, remember?) Don't tell your friends that you're on a ten-day cottage-cheese-and-skim-milk diet; don't ask, "I wonder if I'll make it?"; never mind inquiring as to the caloric content of this or that dish. (You probably already know what is permissible and what isn't, anyway.) Consider your old speech and thinking habits as a detour that you are leaving far behind the smooth highway ahead.

2. Simply accept moderation as a present fact (as if you had asked for something that was immediately granted). Talk and

[3] J. P. Guilford, ed., *Fields of Psychology* (2nd ed.; Princeton, N.J.: D. Van Nostrand Company, Inc., 1950).

act as if past failures have nothing to do with you now (for they really haven't). Believe in success, don't fret, don't worry about results. Quietly accept moderation—or whatever your goal—as your personal property, free from all mortgages. This will become easier and easier as you go along. The strain and struggle will gradually disappear. Oh, there may be a few ups and downs for a while, but it's all part of the game. Remember: *Persistent practice promises progress.*

3. Speak and think success in silence and aloud as often as possible. Say it when you feel like saying it, say it especially when you *don't* feel like saying it, say it when you decline the dessert, say it when you reach for that second helping, say it morning, noon, and night and somewhere in between, say it with all the conviction you can muster, say it when you can muster no conviction at all. Say it, say it, say it!

Professor William James, the prince of American psychologists, urged us to summon all the emotional intensity possible when trying to establish a new habit. Your courageous repetitions cannot fail to sooner or later summon the necessary emotional intensity that will set you up with astounding inner power. Your dominating strengths will then conform to your dominating desires.

In his now-famous book, *The Power of Positive Thinking,* Dr. Norman Vincent Peale offers: "Practice the technique of suggestive articulation, that is, repeat audibly some peaceful words. Words have profound suggestive power, and there is healing in the very saying of them."[4]

And that's why you are invited to the barbecue. You no longer have any reason to fear anything. This is your victory.

YOU MAY APPLY THESE PRINCIPLES ALONE OR WITH A PARTNER

In some cases it would be best to work alone when applying word-power principles, at least until you have made some

[4] Norman Vincent Peale, *The Power of Positive Thinking* (Englewood Cliffs, N.J.: Prentice-Hall, Inc., 1952).

progress. This will protect you from outside negative comments which might tend to lower your enthusiasm.

However, if husband and wife or two friends share equal enthusiasm, they can promote their individual forces by joining forces.

YOU CAN BE A REFRESHING, WINNING PERSON!

Men and women everywhere cry out in anguish of heart, "If I could just be that winning person I want to be! If I could just find some way to start the ball rolling!"

I say this to you:

You *can* be that winning, overcoming, refreshing person. Furthermore, I say to you: *You have already started.* How can I say this? Because you are eager to know, because you are a reasonable seeker, because you just plain want what you want. Since you have already absorbed some of these truths into your consciousness you are already on your way, the ball is now rolling.

I have every confidence that at this very moment a surge of hope—let's call it *faith*—is coursing through you. Somehow, somewhere deep inside, you have that faint but distinct stirring that announces that good things are on their way.

Encourage this feeling right now by repeating the Power Poem, "Things fine are mine!" Say it. Right now. Accept it. Right now. "Things fine are mine!"

You see, God gave you speech for creative purposes. He never gave you *anything* that wasn't good for you, and that certainly includes your powers of speech. "Shout!" cried Joshua to the Israelites at Jericho, "for the Lord hath given you the city." (Joshua 6:16)

The Old Testament also speaks of a man who, "Did it with all his heart, and prospered." (2 Chronicles 31:21)

It's fine old advice for a new man!

HELPFUL HINTS YOU CAN APPLY RIGHT NOW

1. Think of your word-power as a new, exciting adventure that will do great things for you—right now.

2. Remember that speech-strength can be employed anytime, anywhere.

3. Clearly define your goals and desires.

4. Ask for what you want with positive words. Claim them with more positive words!

5. Never doubt, never question, never retreat; simply accept your new verbal-vitalities.

6. Understand that complaining speech increases cause for further complaint, but that cheery, grateful speech multiplies cause for further gratitude.

7. Know that faith is a miracle worker and that faithful words make miracles happen in your life.

8. Talk success and you will soon know what you are talking about!

9. Constantly declare that you are that winning, refreshing person you wish to be.

10. Daily assert, "Things fine are mine!"

HOW DO YOU TALK? ANALYZE YOURSELF!

Chapter 3

A TEACHER ASKED HIS CLASS, "WHAT'S the first thing you do when you sit down to solve a problem in mathematics?"

"Sit down," answered one.

"Take paper and pencil," replied another.

"Give up!" quipped a third.

"The first thing you do," the teacher replied, "is to *look* at it. You closely consider all the ingredients. You ask yourself whether you must add or subtract, divide or multiply. Regardless of the problem, the first logical step is to view it from all angles."

THE HAPPY PURPOSE OF YOUR SELF-ANALYSIS

In the following pages you will be supplied with several techniques which will enable you to clearly see yourself in relation to yourself and your world. You will also learn how to use your word power for making your relations enriching ones. You will be talking about your new self . . . a mighty important topic.

Self-analysis has but this one great final purpose: to enable you to view yourself (psychology calls it *insight* or *awareness*) as *someone else* . . . that someone you yearn to be. Wendell Johnson assures us: "With a fair amount of practice one can become reasonably skilled in observing these characteristics of language behavior in oneself and in others. The ability to recognize them gives one a measure of control over them, and a degree of insight . . ." [1]

Your new awareness will gain you two things: increased life power and decreased insecurity . . . plus all the joys that go with them. Your refreshing inward look will surely bring about that affirmative outlook that will pep up your powers and polish your personality.

BECOME A "TALK-HAWK"

A New Yorker humorously described himself as a new kind of a bird—a "Talk-Hawk"; a sharp-eyed bird that watched everything he said. He reports,

I was very pleased whenever I heard myself saying the right thing, and—oddly enough—it also gave me a thrill whenever I caught myself saying the wrong thing, for I knew that by changing my words I could also change myself.

As I studied my speech habits I found, of course, that they ranged from the jubilant to the dreary. I made a list of both types so I could clearly see what I must retain and what I must banish. My list went like this:

I **will** speak:	I will **not** speak:
patiently	fearfully
spontaneously	suspiciously
gently	indecisively
humorously	sourly
confidently	rigidly
decisively	monotonously
enthusiastically	timidly
forcefully	gloomily
flexibly	critically
calmly	sullenly
authoritatively	angrily
convincingly	pessimistically
modestly	arrogantly
adventurously	fretfully

[1] Wendell Johnson, *People in Quandaries* (New York: Harper and Brothers, 1946).

courageously	hopelessly
tenderly	complainingly

TAKE THESE TWO STEPS

The words (which were also character traits to some extent) which this man discovered are well worth adding to your own list. Use them in this manner:

1. Uncover your negative words just long enough to replace them.
2. Cover yourself with your positive words long enough to make them a permanent part of your personality.

If you now say the wrong things without thinking, your "Talk-Hawk" technique will enable you eventually to say the right things without thinking. This is the sheer beauty of reconditioning your speech habits. Where they once tore you apart without your permission, they now soothe without your prodding. You speak like a new person because you *are* a new person.

EXAMINE YOURSELF JUST LONG ENOUGH TO IDENTIFY CLEARLY THAT WHICH NEEDS REPLACEMENT

Your self-examination calls for no dreary roll-call of your shortcomings. You want no self-scolding, no hopeless review. (You've probably had too much of this already!) You want only to briefly identify your negativity so that you may proceed to talk it away. A doctor never scolds a physical ailment; he examines and treats it. Do likewise! Correct dealing makes for certain healing.

CANCEL YOUR SPEECH POLICY—INSURE YOURSELF ALL OVER

A young life insurance agent once made a sales call upon a psychologist. The psychologist instantly noted that although the young man had his sales technique down pat he lacked that go-getting spark of confidence and enthusiasm so necessary for his line of work. He was hesitant, nervous, unsure of himself. During an awkward pause in the conversation the psychologist's mind quickly caught the interesting parallel between a life insurance policy and a word insurance policy; they had a lot in common. Both were valuable commodities. Both protected the present and offered values for the future. Anyone could insure himself with either, anyone could benefit.

HOW DO YOU TALK TO YOURSELF?

The psychologist felt he could help the young man along in his career, so he ventured, "Do you mind if I ask you a personal question? . . . Tell me, do you speak as convincingly about your policies when you are alone as you do when you are with prospective customers?"

The young man paused a moment, finally replied, "I wouldn't admit this to anyone else but I *do* get discouraged, so naturally I talk that way."

"May I suggest that you write yourself a new kind of a life insurance policy? Cancel your old speech habits and insure yourself all over."

The psychologist then pointed out the parallels between a good life insurance policy and a good speech policy: "Just as you urged me to bring my policy up to date, you must revise your speech habits. I guarantee that if you will cancel out those pessimistic remarks of yours you will also cancel out your discouragement. It's also bound to add extra dollars to your pocket."

DON'T PLAY VERBAL TUG-OF-WAR WITH YOURSELF

The salesman nodded in understanding. "I never thought of it that way before. It just doesn't make sense to talk one way with a client and another way with myself. It's like engaging in a useless tug-of-war with my left and right hands. You can't win."

"Analyze your speech every minute," the psychologist encouraged. "Bring your self-talk in line with your client-talk. Make them exactly the same."

The following month a new personality—but the same salesman—again called at the office. He decisively spoke up: "I've cashed in on that new word policy of mine. I now have all the benefits of self-assurance."

"Fine!" the psychologist congratulated him, "now let's see you go to work on me."

And he did, to the extent of a $20,000 policy.

HOW TO GET RIGHT ANSWERS . . . AND PROFITABLE RESULTS

"The change in your personality is remarkable," said the psychologist as they concluded their business. "Would you mind telling me exactly how you did it?"

The salesman replied, "Between calls, as I drove about, I played a game with myself called Affirmative Answers. I asked countless questions about myself and immediately replied with affirmative answers. And you know, they all turned out to be *right* answers!"

He then wrote out typical questions and answers—which will give you clues for your own procedure:

Questions:	**Affirmative Answers:**
"How are you doing?"	"Excellent! Superb!"
"Expect a successful month?"	"The best of all!"
"What is your daily attitude?"	"Positively terrific!"
"How about your enthusiasm?"	"I'm roaring with it!"
"Are you at ease?"	"My confidence makes ease easy!"

Dr. Norman Vincent Peale confirms the value of this kind of speech when he writes: "Start each day by affirming peaceful, contented, and happy attitudes and your days will tend to be pleasant and successful. Such attitudes are active and definite factors in creating satisfactory conditions. Watch your manner of speech then if you wish to develop a peaceful state of mind."[2]

HOW ABOUT YOUR ANSWERS?

Are you also answering correctly? Are you replying in the way that fills your endeavors with success and satisfaction?

Determine that for every question you will have the right answer—the affirmative one. Follow up every question mark with a positive exclamation point!

EXPAND YOUR CREATIVE ABILITIES BY SPEAKING EXPANSIVELY!

In the last few pages of Chapter 13 I want to give you some details concerning your unlimited opportunities, but for now I'd like to impress you with this single point:

Expansive, free, uninhibited speech paves the way for expansive, unlimited achievements.

You can be only as creative as you are able to *express* creativeness . . . and your language is a major medium of self-expression. The more expression the more expansion, the more expansion the more power.

A university professor illustrated this point by standing before his class with a limp rubber band between his forefinger and thumb. "This rubber band represents your powers of verbal expression. Limp, isn't it? Like to see how easily I turn it into a unit of power?" He stretched the rubber to its full capacity and let it zoom over their heads while quietly observing, "All I did was expand and release it."

So here is your secret for zooming through life:

EXPRESS YOURSELF, EXPAND YOURSELF, AND RELEASE YOURSELF IN NEW CREATIVE POWER

Let me give you a real-life example which will show you exactly how to do this.

[2] Norman Vincent Peale, *The Power of Positive Thinking* (Englewood Cliffs, N.J.: Prentice-Hall, Inc., 1952).

A California woman found employment with a Hollywood talent-and-casting studio. She started near the bottom but made immediate plans for climbing to the top. She had her eyes on a greater income and everything else that would result from a more-than-usual service to her firm.

"From the very start," she relates, "I knew that the principle means I had for selling myself to my superiors was *action.* I had to do bigger things, I had to be inventive, original, progressive. I had to show them I had the stuff.

"But where to start? I looked myself over long enough to discover that my timid speech habits were holding me down. I often said the wrong thing or the ineffective thing or nothing at all. So this was the start; here was where I could remake myself. I had read enough books on personality power to know that folks usually walk the way they talk and vice versa.

"I took the stand that *I was equal in power to every powerful phrase I spoke.* If I *said* that I was creative, I *was* creative; if I *claimed* resourcefulness, I *had great resources at my command.* Now since this was so, all I had to do was to *express* my strength, *believe* in it, and prove it by *acting accordingly.* This idea of making myself the equal of my creative phrases first proved itself when I was given the challenging assignment of getting the contract-signature of an up-and-coming actor. I told myself that it could be done, would be done, and I was the one! This was just the beginning of dozens of large and small achievements that got my career along as I wanted."

GET YOURSELF ALONG!

1. Take the stand that you are equal in creativeness to those creative words you use. Example: since *persistence* is certainly creative, *you* are also persistently creative. Stick by your words until they stick to you.

2. Constantly maintain that the process cannot fail. Believe in it. Accept your equality with your words. The act of believing in them will more and more enable you to recognize your equality.

3. Prove your position and your belief by acting them out at

face value. Even if you doubt, falter, weaken—act them out at face value. In time, you will prove yourself to yourself: your words will prove to be *you.*

DON'T LIMIT YOUR EXPRESSIONS TO WHAT YOU ALREADY KNOW...BUT RATHER KNOW THAT YOU HAVE UNLIMITED EXPRESSION

If your own self-analysis also reveals that your stilted speech patterns are blocking your creative powers, you can use this technique for discovering a new world of self-expression that will surely give you your desired promotions.

Very carefully read this wise observation of Schopenhauer: "Every man takes the limits of his own field of vision for the limits of the world."

Don't let it happen to you! *Please!* Please?

Is it possible that you are now experiencing a life of limited income or limited joy because you believe it is the only world that can exist for you? If so, step out, speak up, enjoy the full measures of blessing that are rightfully yours.

Remember that your speech is a type of action which you can take at this very moment. Decree to yourself, "My vision is unlimited . . . and what I can see I can have. I will therefore see what I can have and have what I can see!"

GIVE YOURSELF A TIME-TEST

It will be helpful if you sometimes specify a definite period of time during which you will play word-detective so that you may track down and arrest all those verbal vagrants. Thirty minutes or an hour is sufficient for this concentrated observation (though you will generally watch yourself all the time). Choose any hour most convenient, keep it to yourself, and play Sherlock Holmes.

As you proceed to analyze your conversations you may be surprised to hear yourself speak in certain ways. This surprise is exactly what you want; it means that you are clearly identifying those little speeches that make or break you.

THE LESS STRAIN, THE MORE GAIN

As with anything else in life, the easy way is always the best way when it comes to self-examination. Casually listen to yourself. Ask yourself if your speech is in harmony with your goals. See whether you can substitute a better word, switch from the depressing to the elevating. Determine whether your phrases are bridges that connect you with your outside world or rivers that separate you.

If and when you catch yourself in a mistake, don't scold yourself; give yourself a pep-talk and replace the ill phrase with a healthy one. Cheer yourself by realizing that a mistake in the present has saved you from twenty in the future. It's a good exchange anytime!

WHAT TO DO WHEN YOU HEAR DEPRESSING AND DISCOURAGING REMARKS FROM OTHERS

You now have some excellent techniques for analyzing your own words as they relate to your daily life. No doubt you have a good measure of confidence that you can carry them through to the point where they will begin to carry you.

"However," someone may remark, "how about those miserable and even cutting remarks from others that I am bound to run into from time to time? How can I employ self-analysis to maintain my feelings of well-being whenever I meet those gloomy folks who never have anything good to say? I certainly want to see myself as a new personality but its hurts like everything when others drop remarks that counter my efforts."

Now it is perfectly true that you cannot always avoid Gloomy Gus. It is not that he has it in for you, it is simply that he is careless, unthinking. He may scarcely recognize his miserable utterances as negative influences, but they subtly penetrate your feelings. The human mind is amazingly receptive to suggestions, even to untrue ones. (For example, perhaps you have seen folks under the control of hypnotic suggestion who were unable to raise their arms because the hypnotist merely *sug-*

gested that they couldn't—but when the basically untrue suggestion was removed they were free to function normally).

SWITCH TO THE POSITIVE!

Robert Southwell points out, "What thought can think, another thought can mend." We might add, "What word can destroy, another word can establish."

The very next time you run into a miserable utterance that seems to threaten your well-being, immediately call into action a countering influence. Turn on your positive speaking, your affirmative thinking, your religious faith, your prayer power and anything else that supports your rightful position. Do it deliberately, quietly, with unabashed frankness.

You cannot afford to do otherwise. You simply cannot maintain a sense of worthiness if you meekly accept negative opinions about yourself. Remember—if they disturb you even slightly they have entered with emotional force. The longer you allow them to remain inside, the more they will spread. You may think you can pass them off with a bit of quiet suffering but you are not built that way. We are always doing things to our self-esteem—either elevating it or allowing it to droop.

DON'T RUN YOURSELF DOWN!

Never—*never*—run yourself down. Never express yourself as being inferior, for if you do, you will believe what you say and your belief makes it so.

Carefully watch both your public and inner speech. Forbid your tongue to slip one over on you with phrases such as, "I am not as capable as others," and, "My best is not good enough," and, "I'll probably blunder."

Instead, express opposite phrases that charge you with confidence . . . and your belief in confidence makes it so.

Gloomy Gus will never bother you again once you understand that:

YOUR **FEELINGS** ABOUT YOUR CAPABILITIES MAY BE TEMPORARILY DISTURBED, BUT YOUR **BASIC WORTH** IS UNTOUCHABLE

A clergyman illustrates this truth by telling of a boyhood experience: "During a baseball game I dropped a fly ball, after which a teammate named Steve called me a 'big ox.' Naturally, it hurt. When I got home and mentioned it to my father, he told me to bring him the dictionary."

"Here we are," said my father as he opened the book, "the dictionary defines an ox as a *male bovine quadruped.*" He looked up. "Are you a male bovine quadruped?"

I frowned. What's *that?*"

"That's a big ox. You know, a big clumsy animal that wanders around the pasture munching grass."

My frown deepened. "What's that got to do with me?"

"Nothing. And that's just the point. Are you a big clumsy animal that wanders around the pasture munching grass?"

It was my turn to give him a curious once-over. "Of course not. I'm a . . . a *boy.*"

"Then you're definitely not a big ox?"

CORRECTLY DEFINE YOURSELF

"Of course I'm not a big ox."

"Then why get mad when someone calls you something that you are not? Don't you see, son? You got mad when Steve called you that name because you sort of *believed* what he said."

"I guess so."

"He hurt your feelings because he made you feel like an ox. But the feeling was false. You are not a big ox, you are just a baseball player who dropped the ball. Correctly analyze yourself; see the difference in the two."

I felt better. "That makes sense," I agreed.

"The only thing you should feel is that you are a boy who dropped a ball. A boy who made a very common error. Look at it impersonally for a while and you'll see that you can control your feelings by maintaining your rights, by insisting on what you really are. Don't ever allow anyone to convince you of anything else."

DENY FALSE APPRAISALS

The next day I scribbled a note and slipped it to Steve during class. He stared at me in puzzlement for a minute. When the light finally dawned, he grinned at me.

That note has had a profound influence on my everyday peace of mind. It read:

> "Steve:
> I am *not* a *male bovine quadruped.*
> And that's *that.*"

WHEN OPINIONS DISTURB YOU ...

Semantics, the science of language, tells us that we mistakenly accept a symbol—a word—as the object itself. But a mere word is not the object itself.

So do this the very next time a spoken opinion disturbs you: Carefully examine it for accuracy. If it points out a simple human shortcoming, gratefully use it as a means for self-improvement. If it incorrectly describes you, replace it with the true and worthy self-description. If you are frank and fearless in this, you will be frank and fearless in every situation. A true self-analysis frees you from the agony of false opinion.

"THAT CANNOT POSSIBLY BE TRUE"

Let me tell you of a man who developed a fine method for correctly analyzing himself.

Wherever he encountered negativity—at the office, in the sly slams of fear-advertising, even in his own reflections—he immediately denied it. Regardless of how deep the painful impression, he immediately rejected the implication that it had power to hurt him. And once the denial was made he forgot the whole thing. He kept a record of his phraseology so that he might check it for both firmness and courtesy. The following examples are somewhat formalized, but here is the idea:

"That cannot possibly be true."

"Sorry, I just don't believe it."

"No."

"I refuse to accept that opinion."

"I cannot agree."

"That is an incorrect appraisal."

BEST OF ALL...

He was delightfully surprised to find that the longer he practiced self-acceptance the less need he found for defending himself. Why? Because his own mounting assurance of his true worth automatically edged out his touchiness and sensitivity to the opinions of others.

ASSERT YOUR TRUE POWERS

How would you like to live in that peaceful state where nothing can disturb you, where people will wonder at your sweet and strong nature? You can surely attain this state by convincing yourself of a profound truth about yourself. This truth is: *Nothing in life has power to disturb you. Nothing!* If you are disturbed it is simply because you have given people and circumstances a false power over you. Get rid of these arrogant authorities by decreeing:

"I am absolutely untouchable. No one in the world has the ability to distress me. Regardless of any temporary upset, I continue to assert my true powers of tranquillity and self-respect. I need never become angry or suspicious of anything, I need only to understand that in God's sight and in my own sight I am untouchable. Since this is a Divine truth I can easily afford to be kind, gentle, and loving at all times."

This is so vital to your life-welfare that I would like you to read it over and think it through several times. Reword it in any way you like, but absorb it into your consciousness once and for all. And once and for all you will be at peace.

IN REALITY, YOU POSSESS UNSHAKEABLE DIGNITY

When we face reality, when we really believe that we are human beings possessed of unassailable dignity, we no longer find it necessary to dodge verbal spears which others may hurl at us. Our warm understanding melts them like ice long before they can penetrate.

When we replace untrue estimates with ones of affirmation of our rightful place we are only obeying God's law, for He holds us in the highest possible esteem.

The apostle Paul declares of mankind, "Thou crownedst him with glory and honour, and didst set him over the works of thy hands." (Hebrews 2:7)

Honor *does* belong to you.

Will you accept it?

REMEMBER THESE LIFE-GIVING SUGGESTIONS

1. Frankly, honestly, and effortlessly examine your daily speech habits.

2. Know that self-analysis is a good step toward self-elevation.

3. Be a "Talk-Hawk."

4. Make it a policy to insure your life with affirmative language in all circumstances.

5. Consistently expand the manner in which you express yourself. Say something new, refreshing, adventurous.

6. Break through those vicious verbal circles at every opportunity.

7. Declare and believe that your life visions are without limit. Look beyond yourself, act beyond yourself . . . and you will find yourself with limitless opportunities.

8. Refuse to absorb, refuse to believe unjust and unworthy opinions about yourself.

9. Replace negative opinions with positive facts.

10. Know that you now possess unshakeable dignity. Believe it and you will experience a peaceful stability at all times.

SPEECH SECRETS THAT WILL CHANGE YOUR LIFE

Chapter 4

DO YOU KNOW THAT YOU HAVE A SEcret power?

You use it every minute, a thousand times a day. It controls your speech, your actions, your emotions, and everything else that sums up your personality.

It makes you do things you want to do. It also makes you do things you don't want to do. It makes you mysteriously elated or downhearted, even when you can see no reason for either emotion.

It is a power that either controls you or is controlled by you. Like electricity, it can be harnessed and used for daily benefits, but if you allow it to run wild it will cause you to run emotionally wild.

YOUR SECRET POWER CAN BE TURNED INTO YOUR OBEDIENT SERVANT

I want to let you in on this secret power. When you know it as a *revealed* power it will work daily miracles in your everyday life. It will serve to turn your difficulties into triumphs.

Let's take our first look at it with an illustration that may sound somewhat familiar to you:

SAM RUNS INTO A DIFFICULTY . . .

The pastor of a small church in a mountain community and one of his parishioners—whom we'll call Short-tempered Sam—set off one morning for a few hours of relaxed fishing. They intended using a small boat which was jointly owned by the men-folk of the church and which was moored by the lake for the convenience of all who cared to use it.

Upon their arrival they found that the previous fisherman had jammed the craft against some rocks, damaging it to the extent that it was half-filled with water.

AND THE DIFFICULTY RUNS INTO SAM . . .

"Some people!" Sam viciously exploded. "Here we come out for a few hours of rest and run into this mess. *Some* people!"

"Disappointing, isn't it?" remarked his pastor. "But let's see if we can fix things up."

Sam continued to grumble as they rowed the repaired boat to the center of the lake so the pastor tried to calm him down with, "Forget it, Sam. It's a beautiful day; the fish are biting. Forget it."

Sam again muttered something about "inconsiderate people" and sputtered, "Look, pastor, it's all right for *you* to sit there and advise me to cool off; that's your job. But *me*, I'm just a tense, hard-driving businessman who needs to explode every once in a while." He shrugged and added, "You're the calm type and I'm not . . . as simple as that."

LEARN TO CORRECT YOUR VERBAL RESPONSES AND YOU'LL BE CALM IN ANY SITUATION

"You can learn to be calm in any situation," the pastor remarked, "once you learn to correct your word responses. Most of us get mad in little things like this because we feel ourselves under personal attack. As odd as it seems, we actually believe that someone or something is out to get us, to annoy, to take advantage of us. So we explode with angry words—and blow ourselves up."

The pastor paused long enough to tug on his line. "Sam, just suppose we had found a note in the boat from Charlie Green saying he had accidentally damaged the boat and was sorry for any inconvenience it had caused us. Would that change your attitude toward the situation?"

Sam nodded. "Sure it would. It makes a lot of difference when you understand things as they actually are. Charlie wouldn't deliberately spoil anyone's fun."

REFUSE TO BELIEVE IN PERSONAL OFFENSE—DON'T EXPRESS PERSONAL OFFENSE—AND YOU WILL NEVER EXPERIENCE IT

"You see," said the pastor, "when you take the attitude that there is no personal offense the whole thing becomes easy. If you had just made this *no-offense* response from the very start you would have saved yourself all that fuss."

"I'll have to agree to that."

The pastor reached into a jacket pocket and pulled out a note which he read aloud: "'Sorry I blundered. Will repair boat this afternoon.'" The pastor added, "It's signed by Charlie Green. I found it tucked in a crack."

Sam sat in silent understanding as the pastor continued.

"If you will learn to respond correctly—with patient speech—you will free your mind from all suspicions that anyone or anything is attacking your rights—and you will be calm in every difficult circumstance. I guarantee this to be the absolute truth. It's amazing how much trouble we can avoid simply by *impersonalizing*, by refusing to believe in attack."

Dr. John A. Schindler remarked: "It is hard to conceive of a single irritation, at least in the usual run of things, that *ever needs* to get under one's skin."[1]

[1] John A. Schindler, *How to Live 365 Days a Year* (Englewood Cliffs, N.J.: Prentice-Hall, Inc., 1955).

IMPERSONALIZE THE UNHAPPY, PERSONALIZE THE HAPPY!

If you will also practice the fine art of impersonalizing unpleasant circumstances—and personalizing pleasant ones—you will soon be making *new* responses, you will charge yourself with an unlimited amount of delightful characteristics that will draw folks to you.

SO THIS IS YOUR SECRET POWER—THE POWER TO RESPOND **CORRECTLY**

Psychology tells us that Sam's angry outburst is nothing more than a learned response. It is something he learned to do; in other words, a habit (a habit which can be changed). It is certainly *not* some unpleasant characteristic he inherited from his father. In their book *Psychology,* Robert S. Woodworth and Donald G. Marquis sum up: "All knowledge and skill, all habits good and bad, all acquaintance with people and things, all attitudes built up in your dealing with people and things, have been learned."[2]

Therefore, anything of an unpleasant nature that has been learned can also be *unlearned* and *replaced* with pleasant characteristics.

If you also find yourself responding angrily when you really want to respond kindly or courageously or cheerfully, don't worry about it. It is enough to know that the very same power that now upsets you can also be turned toward the happy and constructive. You see, *a negative response can always be switched to a positive one!*

THINK WHAT THIS MEANS TO YOU!

What a fantastic truth! It means that you can actually, literally, once-and-for-all remake yourself into the kind of person

[2] Robert S. Woodworth and Donald G. Marquis, Psychology, 5th ed. (New York: Henry Holt & Company, Inc., 1947).

you want to be. *Any* poor habit can be turned into a good habit, any timid reaction can be switched to a courageous one. If you have the power of speech, you have the power to change.

WRITE DOWN A "NEVER AGAIN" LIST

Now that you have an idea of what hostile and discouraging speech does to you, write down a "never again" list. Vow, "Never again will I speak *in* defeat, *of* limitation, *with* suspicion, *for* spite."

Vow it. Mean it. Practice it. And you will never again be bothered with defeat, limitation, suspicion, spite. None of the ripples of life can soak you unless you leap in panic from the boat.

TO CHANGE YOUR RESPONSES, CHANGE YOUR WORDS

I'd like you to continue to change your responses to life. Please read the following truth-statements slowly and convincingly. Read them with authority, for you now *have* the authority, you are in charge of the powerhouse. Read them as if they personally apply to you, for they do.

"I dwell in inner security as a habit just as I dwell securely in my home as a habit."

"I walk in love as a habit just as I walk down the street as a habit."

"I drink spiritual refreshment as a habit just as I drink water as a habit."

"I enjoy good health as a habit just as I enjoy good music as a habit."

"I wear peace of mind as a habit just as I wear clothing as a habit."

REFRESHING RESPONSES ARE NOW SURGING THROUGH YOU

Whether you are now conscious of it or not, you have just now taken a plunge into a refreshing atmosphere. Remember? . . . your *words* change *you*. You will *feel* the change in a very real way in due time.

DON'T BLAME YOURSELF—EXAMINE YOURSELF

Have you ever said, "I don't *want* to be depressed, I just can't help it," or "I didn't *mean* to say that unworthy thing, it just slipped out"?

Of course. No one wants to be weak or timid or impulsive or anything else unworthy of the best that is in him. No one *really* wants to be that way, but some people are that way because they can do nothing else; their destructive responses are simply a solid part of their learned personality habits. But no one, including yourself, need blame himself for being where he is . . . as long as he is trying to change his residence.

POSITIVE WORDS ARE ELEVATORS. ARE YOU GOING UP?

If you are stuck in the basement of life it is possible that you have not been using your words as life-elevators. I want you to know that you can use your word power to elevate yourself to the tenth, twentieth, thirtieth stories of your life-building. Even to fortieth and fiftieth stories which you may not presently see!

Call out your floor with elevating speech! Visualize yourself as actually going up whenever you declare, "I'm alive to life!" and, "I appreciate your friendship!"

Likewise, see yourself as stranded whenever you groan, "I'm stuck with life," and, "My circumstances are hopeless."

If you will actually practice this elevator method you will catch a clearer view of what your speech does for—or against—you. I doubt that you will want to remain in the basement by speaking lowly words.

HOW TO RECOGNIZE DEFEATISM WHEN YOU HEAR IT

Perhaps you want more detail. Perhaps you ask, "Exactly what words are wrong ones? Which ones should I avoid?"

The answer is simply: *All words that you don't want to be translated into your life as personal experiences.*

If you don't want weakness, don't describe yourself as weak; if you are tired of frustration, avoid frustrated talk; if you are sick of ill health, don't harp about it; if you don't want gloom, cut out gloomy speech.

It is really as elementary as that. To dismiss grief from your life you must first dismiss it from your vocabulary.

IMPORTANT! READ THE FOLLOWING VERY CAREFULLY!

Now it is obvious that *all positive words should have a positive meaning to you.* By this I mean that good words should excite good feelings, energetic responses. They should fill you with faith, hope, ambition, and all other dynamic powers.

But *do* they? Make this test: Does the word *happiness* really mean your rightful portion in life? . . . or does it secretly mean something always around the corner? What does the word *wealth* mean to you?—a Divinely promised reward for properly using your talents? . . . or an elusive treasure found only by the "lucky"?

Happiness and wealth are positive words and should cause you to respond positively, but—face this frankly—do they induce instead a response or an attitude of doubt, cynicism, suspicion?

If so, you have found the answer! You can now know that your negative responses to positive words are making it impossible for the wonderful Laws of Life to supply you with those riches you desire . . . *and that positive responses to positive words will make an abundant supply possible!*

Constantly remember, if you respond with a "no" when you should say "yes," you are saying "no" to success. When you speak negatively about positive things—such as happiness and wealth—you turn them into negative things *as far as you are concerned.*

CHANGE ALL THIS!

Turn handsprings! You will change all this! No longer have any doubts or suspicions or timidities toward anything good you desire. Associate good words with a good life. Believe that you can *live* happiness, *attain* wealth. These right beliefs in right words will surely draw right things to you. You will be positively dazzled at your new brilliance.

HOW YOU CAN CHANGE POSITIVE WORDS INTO THEIR RIGHTFUL, POSITIVE MEANINGS

I want to tell you a humorous story that has a serious application to the above vital ideas. It will show you how to correctly associate with positive words. As you read, bear in mind that *your goal is to banish all negative responses from your positive words.*

STEP BOLDLY UP TO YOUR AMBITION

On a small farm in the Middle West there once lived a very sweet little old lady. Her lifelong ambition was to become—of all things—a lion-tamer! So when the circus came to town one Monday morning she set her knitting aside and approached the circus manager.

"Young man," she frankly spoke up, "I'd like to become a lion-tamer."

The manager slid off his chair—*thump*—he hit the sawdust. "Would you mind repeating that?" he asked as he sat there smacking his ear.

"I said," she sweetly repeated, "that I'd like to become a lion-tamer."

He dragged himself to his feet. "But . . . but *Granny,*" he shakily gasped, "you just don't walk up and say that you want to tame lions. Least of all a sweet little old lady like you."

"Why not?" she innocently asked.

"Why . . . why . . ." he flustered, "you just *don't.* Perhaps you are not aware that lions are dangerous beasts to associate with." As she firmly stood her ground he weakly gestured and said, "Look, Grandma, we *could* use someone to sell the popcorn. Maybe you . . ."

STICK TO IT!

Granny tightly pressed her lips together and replied, "A lion-tamer or nothing!"

The manager drew a deep breath and gestured toward a chair. "Sit down, Granny, and let me explain a few things to you. Do you know what would happen if you started associating with lions?"

"No," she replied, "because I've never done it before."

"All right," he groaned, "tell you what. I'll give you a free pass so that you can come over every day and watch our expert lion-tamer at work." He confidently smiled. "But I don't imagine you'll be back tomorrow."

KEEP COMING BACK TO ALL THOSE "FEARFUL LIONS"
(Positive Words Which Induce a Negative Attitude)

But bright and early the next day Granny cheerfully stepped up to where the chief lion-tamer was snapping his lions through their paces. "Young man," she said, "may I associate with your lions?"

The whip dropped from his hand. "Granny," he gasped, "you just don't cheerfully walk up and state that you want to associate with lions. Lions are very savage beasts you know."

"*You* handle them, don't you?" she quietly asked.

"Yes, but that's different . . . I've been associating with them for years."

"Ah!" she exclaimed with a triumphant smile, "you learned to do by doing. Why can't I do the same?"

He groaned. "Well . . . I'll tell you what. Here, take this

whip. Stand outside the cage and watch me. Masterfully flick your whip about just as I do."

So for the rest of the day Granny acted just like the lion-tamer acted. She stood outside the cage and commanded, "Up, Nero! Down, Caesar!"

HABITUAL ASSOCIATION BUILDS HABITUAL CONFIDENCE

The next morning Granny again politely addressed the lion-tamer. "Please, sir, today I would like to step *inside* the cage so I might have a closer association with those savage beasts." She added, "Yesterday's practice certainly gives me worlds of new confidence."

"But Granny," he objected, "grannies are grannies and lion-tamers are lion-tamers. How can you be both?"

She gently smiled. "Just open the cage and you'll find out!"

He reluctantly permitted her to enter. "But stay near the gate," he warned, "lions gobble up grannies."

Throughout the day she more closely associated with all the savage lions. "You know," she exclaimed, "the closer I get the braver I get!"

The third day she requested, "Please, sir, I would now like to stick my head inside the lion's mouth." And before he could object she did just that.

"Didn't it frighten you?" asked the amazed lion-tamer.

"Not in the slightest," she replied. "But I do suggest you buy Nero some of those breath-sweetening tablets."

On the fourth day the circus manager walked up—and almost dropped his roll of free passes. "What?" he choked, "are my eyes deceiving me or is that Granny in the lion's den?"

"It's not Daniel," sighed the lion-tamer.

"But how? . . . how did she do it?"

"She has some funny business she calls *association.*"

The manager gazed in sheer admiration as Granny put the savage lions through their paces. "Granny is no longer just a granny," he exclaimed, "she's an expert lion-tamer! Look how she responds to the lions . . . look how they respond to her!"

He suddenly frowned. "I *still* don't get it. By no rule in the book can a granny become a tamer of savage beasts."

WRITE SOME NEW RULES

"I told you," the lion-tamer sheepishly replied, "it's not *in* the book . . . it's just a matter of getting acquainted."

"Granny," the manager called through the bars, "you're one in a million!"

"No," she corrected, "I just had a million confidences that I could do this one thing."

SNAP YOUR VERBAL WHIP AND YOU'LL TAME ALL THOSE "NEGATIVE LIONS" IN YOUR LIFE

I'm not suggesting that you rush out to the nearest circus, but I do know that Granny's triumph would be a good thing to remember. If you also wish to master life, take these eight steps:

1. Make a list of those lionlike (fearful and unhappy) words in your life. Determine just which ones induce timid or confused responses. Could it be *love? Men? Women? Learning? Money? Security? Friendship?* Write them down.

2. Get acquainted with their *real* meanings. Know that they *need not* mean savagery to you. Know that a verbal lion is uncontrollable only because you don't fully understand it, because you have previously spoken and acted as if it were uncontrollable. It will help you here to think of a word that frightened you at one time but that you now confidently handle. For example, does *ghost* now scare you? Of course not, for you now know it describes a nonexistent creature. Does *thunder* cause you to cringe? No, it even gives you a thrill—for you understand it to be a natural phenomenon. Now consider that you will likewise grow into the rightful understanding of your present lionlike words.

3. Associate constantly with your verbal lions and their life equivalents. Do this by speaking them, reading about them, enjoying them. Realize that the more association the less fear-

some they will become to you. Snap your mental whip at them —watch them cower!

4. Bear in mind at all times that you are the masterful lion-tamer. Pay no attention to your own emotional snarls whenever you hear them.

5. Practice lionlike words—and their life equivalents—at every opportunity. For instance, take the word *indecision.* How do you banish indecision? By practicing *decision.* So practice it, perhaps in small ways at first. Don't think so hard: act instead. Take the word *acceptance.* Want to be accepted? *Act* as if you *are* accepted, regardless of what you *think* about it. Talk to everyone you meet just as if each one fully appreciates you. Whatever your lionlike word, *practice its affirmative meaning.* You will soon be *living* what you have been practicing.

6. Whenever possible, associate the unfamiliar with the familiar. What a wonderful way to make the unfamiliar the familiar! Suppose, for example, your lionlike word is *shyness.* All right, you are shy. But you are not, you know, shy with everyone; there are at least a few close friends or relatives with whom you are at ease. Here's what to do: Tell yourself that people are people, that if you are at ease at home you are at ease with strangers. You see, *ease is already a part of you,* so carry it with you wherever you go, pretend that it is impossible to lose it. You will find that this will be so. Carry your familiar self into all unfamiliar situations.

7. Keep an interested eye on yourself as you proceed. Look inside yourself for those ever-so-slight (yet quite definite) changes for the better. You may notice, for example, that *acceptance* is becoming more than a word—it is gradually revealing itself as a reality in your social contacts. It is important —and thrilling!—to become aware of these steady switches from the negative to the positive, for they will skyrocket your faith in even greater improvements. You will see that when a lionlike word or circumstance becomes a positive mental habit it turns into a gentle rabbit.

8. "Practice yourself, for heaven's sake, in little things; and thence proceed to greater," advises Epictetus.

POWER-PACKED SPEECH MEANS POWER-PACKED EXPERIENCES!

Let me supply you with another dynamic idea for translating all of your power-packed words into power-packed victories. Sound like a good idea? Believe me, it is!

You have seen that your words must always be to you exactly what you *believe* them to be to you (faith, again!). If happiness means something unattainable, you yourself translate it into an unattainable experience. If courage means the ability to get out, get up, get over, that's exactly the way you will translate it into your daily endeavors. You reap what you verbally sow, you collect what you expect.

So . . .

GIVE YOUR POSITIVE WORDS A PERSONAL MEANING —AND MAKE THEM MEAN WHAT THEY SAY

Here is the lively thing you want to do with those positive words you speak:

You want them to personally mean exactly what they are supposed to mean.

So make the word *happiness* mean just one thing to you . . . *your life happiness.*

Make the word *courage* reveal itself as . . . *personal courage in all your endeavors.*

Determine that the word *radiance* will mean . . . *your radiance of personality.*

Interpret the word *progress* as . . . *your constant progress.*

Here is a story that will illustrate this idea:

"THINGS COULDN'T BE WORSE!" COMPLAINED THE RICH MAN

A wealthy acquaintance of mine once paid me a visit during his vacation. As we sat on the sofa he opened the conversation with the gloomy lament, "Things couldn't be worse."

This surprised me for I knew his business was booming and his social life was all that one might wish.

"You can't quite put your finger on it, can you?" I remarked.

"That's just it!" he complained. "Here I am a man of wealth and position, but how do I feel? Just plain depressed. What's it all about?"

"Tom," I told him, "you often take certain business risks in order to gain a profit. Will you risk putting yourself in my hands for a few minutes? Will you do as I ask?"

"What can I lose?" he sighed. "Go ahead."

"All right," I challenged him, "from this moment on I want you to do just two things. First, I want you to speak cheerfully. Second, I want you to make your cheery words mean exactly what they say. In other words, *personalize* them. I want you to associate your own feelings with the very meanings of those words. A cheery word means that *you* are cheery, a decisive word means that *you* are decisive. Don't ever again think of happiness as something only for your neighbor. Just as often as possible associate your words with yourself. Form an intimate union with them."

"Sounds like a good risk," he agreed.

"To put it another way," I continued, "start thinking of the word meanings as your personal property. Start claiming them. Speak and think of them as your intimate experiences."

Puzzled, he asked, "Right now? . . . before I actually have them as my personal property?"

STAKE YOUR CLAIM!

"Yes. Right *now*. Stake your claim to all that gold; I assure you that it is there right now waiting for you to dig it up." I handed him a list of suitable affirmations. "Here, read these, start digging."

He read aloud:

"Happiness means happiness for *me*."

"Courage means *personal* courage."

"I translate relaxation as *my* relaxation."

"Patience is always a *personal* characteristic."

"Love means *my* love."

"Self-control means *personal* self-control."

"Cheeriness means *me*."

He left with the promise to faithfully work on the two pointers I had supplied. When he returned on the last day of his stay in town his life attitude was completely reversed.

"It worked, didn't it?" I said, noting his smile.

"Did it!" he shouted. "With your permission, I'm printing these affirmations in our company paper. We'll not only have the most skilled employees in town but the cheeriest. If anyone doubts that it works I'll call him up to my office for a personal testimony."

He paused a moment and made an admission, "It's funny, but when you first told me about these speech secrets I had my doubts. I didn't see how in the world such a commonplace thing as *talking* could have any secrets to it. But when I saw how personalized speech creates personalized feelings . . . well . . . what a secret!"

Make it *your* secret!

In his scientific book on happiness-building, *Autoconditioning*, Dr. Hornell Hart follows up a discussion of personalized word-use with: "You find that you are building a new set of attitudes and habits. A new way of life begins to take possession of you—courageous, friendly, and receptive." [3]

NAME IT AND CLAIM IT!

The great Bible saints and heroes knew this secret long before my wealthy friend did. They hesitated not a moment to personally claim all of God's goodnesses, many of them the very same good things that you now seek. Hundreds of beautiful Bible passages proclaim the intimate union of the seeker with the sought. They claim, "*My* joy, *my* hope, *my* peace."

Now you may be neither saint nor hero, but God never withholds His gifts because of imperfections in human goodness.

He "giveth to all men liberally." (James 1:5)

[3] Hornell Hart, *Autoconditioning* (Englewood Cliffs, N.J.: Prentice-Hall, Inc., 1956).

Your part is to liberally claim.
This secret will surely change your life.
But your part is to liberally claim.

TEN SECRETS FOR DAILY VICTORY

1. Practice the affirmative verbal response in every situation . . . and you will live affirmatively in every situation.

2. Impersonalize the unhappy; personalize the happy.

3. Accept pleasurable feelings as a personal habit, just as you accept any other personal habit.

4. Realize that at this very moment your word power is doing great things for you!

5. See yourself as ascending higher and higher in life when you speak elevating words.

6. Make positive words mean positive living!

7. Step up to—and stick to—your goals.

8. Turn those fearful words—and their life equivalents—into winning experiences.

9. Remember that you are the master of your speech habits, your circumstances, and yourself.

10. Make every successful word mean your success.

BELIEVE IN YOURSELF — FAITH POWER THROUGH WORD POWER

Chapter 5

PROBABLY THE TWO GREAT QUESTIONS most folks ask about faith are:

"What is it?"

"How can I use it?"

In regard to the first question, you should know that no man can ever define faith to another. The dictionary can only supply a few synonyms such as *confidence* and *trust.*

Faith cannot be verbally defined, it can only be experienced. This should be marvelous news for you if you are seeking to draw life's goodness, for this chapter will take you step by step to the point where you can experimentally define faith. You see, you can only define faith to yourself, and you do so in terms of experience.

FAITH IS WHAT YOU ARE, FAITH IS HOW YOU TALK, FAITH IS HOW YOU LIVE, FAITH IS ACTION . . . NOT MERELY AN ISOLATED PRINCIPLE

Whenever you want to do something but think that you haven't enough faith to carry it through, do this:

First do it without faith—and the time will come when you will do it *with* faith . . . and do it much better.

Understand that action produces faith and that faith induces action. Keep this idea clear by thinking of Faith and Action as two lively schoolboys who race hand-in-hand, each taking turns at swinging the other forward.

A young squirrel who eagerly wanted to climb to the top of his first tree in order to enjoy the wide, wonderful world asked his mother, "How do I get faith enough to climb this tree?"

"Do it," she said.

"But what if I slip?"

"Do it."

"But what if I trip?"

"Do it."

"But what if I flip?"

"Do it."

So he did it . . . and *did* it. From that day forth he had an eager faith that he could climb *any* tree. And he did.

The rest of this chapter is devoted to fully answering the second question, to showing you how you can make faith a practical power in your life.

AT THIS VERY MOMENT YOU HAVE A MEASURE OF FAITH . . . SO TAKE IT FROM HERE

The very fact that you are now reading this chapter is ample evidence that you have at least an elementary faith in faith. You *do* believe in possibilities for greater things; you have confidence that there is a way. It is all you need for the present. You are never asked for the impossible.

DECLARE YOUR FAITH!

It is essential that you start declaring your faith, no matter how little you feel you have. The Bible declares that a mustard-seed faith will move mountains; it doesn't ask for a mountain-like faith to move a mustard seed.

A little is a lot when it comes to faith power. But you must use the little you have if you want mountains to eventually move.

We have spoken of the necessity of combining our faith with action. As Kenneth Hildebrand comments: "But faith cannot become 'tested power' for us until we venture on it in the practical affairs of life. Psychologists point out that both belief and doubt are living attitudes, and involve *conduct*. We express belief or doubt by living accordingly."[1]

It is obvious that our words involve attitudes and conduct —they *are* attitudes and conduct, they are a man's faith-in-action. It is again obvious that we can get ourselves into some uplifting actions by starting with activating (faithfully positive) words.

BE YOUR OWN MAGICIAN

Many years ago in a far-away land there once lived a young prince named Paulus. Paulus was an alert and intélligent young prince, but alas, was possessed of a frail and puny body. So weak and sickly was he that everyone gave him the title of the "Puny Prince." Puny Prince Paulus bathed in magic waters and hopped on his left foot in the moonlight, but nothing seemed to help his puny nature. In despair, he fell before his father, the wise king who sat on his throne.

"Father," pleaded the Puny Prince, "please give me a magic brew so that I might become a Powerful Prince."

The wise king shook his head. "I have no magic, my son. You must be your own magician."

"But father," cried the Puny Prince as he bowed his head in grief and bewilderment, "many, many times I have tried to help myself but always I fail."

His father kindly smiled. "Prince Paulus, there is power of which you have not heard. But you must promise to faithfully carry out my instructions."

"*Anything,*" promised his son. "Tell me of this magic."

"SEEING IS BELIEVING" . . . **SAYING** IS BELIEVING

"Very well," the wise king replied. "You must stand on the palace steps and proclaim five times to the people that you are a Powerful Prince."

[1] Kenneth Hildebrand, *Achieving Real Happiness* (New York: Harper and Brothers, 1953).

"Go on," the Puny Prince eagerly exclaimed, "what else must I do?"

"That is all. Faithfully proclaim five times that you are a Powerful Prince."

The young prince frowned. "That is *all?*"

The wise king nodded. "That is all. But be very sure that you faithfully obey my exact counsel."

VOICE YOUR CHOICE

The eager young prince raced to the palace steps. "I am a Powerful Prince!" he shouted to the waiting throng, then doubtfully added, "At least I *guess* I am."

"You have not fully obeyed my wise command," said his observing father. "Try again."

"I am a Powerful Prince!" he exclaimed, but instantly turned to his father with the gloomy remark, "But I don't *feel* like one."

"Forget your feelings, son. Try again."

"I am a Powerful Prince!" he shouted once more but miserably muttered under his breath as he peered outward, "My subjects are laughing at me."

"You must not listen to their scorn," advised the wise king. "Close your ears and open your mouth."

"I am a Powerful Prince!" he announced, but sadly added, "It doesn't seem to work."

"Try again. Do exactly as I have advised."

"I am a Powerful Prince!" he shouted for the fifth time, but sadly whispered, "I believe I have failed again."

"My son," the wise king said as he laid gentle hands on the young prince's shoulders, "you must not listen to your feelings, you must not be influenced by the crowd, you must not believe in disbelief. You must listen only to your declarations of faith."

PERSISTENT REPETITION IS FAITH-IN-ACTION

The young prince thoughtfully nodded. "I understand at last. I must express pure faith with pure declarations."

Said the wise king as he departed, "A steady persistence in truth will give you a ready insistence in truth. And then wonderful things start to happen."

The young prince boldly stood before the multitude and proclaimed:

"*I* am a Powerful Prince!"
"I *am* a Powerful Prince!"
"I am *a* Powerful Prince!"
"I am a *Powerful* Prince!"
"I am a Powerful *Prince!*"

As he stood there he began to feel a strange surge of power. His legs grew steady, his shoulders straightened, his head proudly lifted. The multitude curiously muttered, "Something wonderful is happening to our prince. See how noble, how powerful he is!"

From that day forth they gave him the new title of the Powerful Prince.

Because he *was* as he faithfully *declared* he was.

What do you suppose were the inner speakings of Henry Ford as he experimented with mechanics? Perhaps something like: "I am the builder of a successful automobile." Could he have continued to the end had he *not* constantly declared his faith in himself? Of course not. What do you imagine Luther Burbank declared as he worked in his gardens? Quite likely: "I am the creator of a superior potato." In due time he was that which he declared of himself—a botanical miracle-man. You can think of countless folks of today who became prominent and wealthy by courageously declaring their faith in their abilities.

"HOW TO DO IT"

Your Bible is abundant with messages that confirm your present abilities and opportunities to attain full measures of power-giving faith.

"It may sound like an unusual definition of the Bible," a missionary said, "but when you come right down to it the Bible is the world's most accurate how-to-do-it book."

He referred to passages such as:

"Faith cometh by hearing, and hearing by the word of God." (Romans 10:17) Which means that whenever you hear or speak faithful words you are instilling yourself with faith.

"Faith is the substance of things hoped for, the evidence of things not seen." (Hebrews 11:1) Which means that you must spiritually see that which you desire before your physical eyes can see it.

"A faithful man shall abound with blessings." (Proverbs 28:20) Which means exactly what it says!

COOPERATE WITH YOUR FAITH AND IT WILL OPERATE FOR YOU

Little Billy asked his Sunday school teacher if it were really true that faith could move mountains.

"The Bible says exactly that," he was informed.

"You mean," Billy persisted, "that with enough faith I can actually move that mountain in back of the church?"

"Yes."

When Billy started to leave the classroom his teacher asked him where he was going.

"To get a shovel and move that mountain."

"But you need faith, not a shovel."

"I know," Billy called back as he shot around a corner, "but I imagine some cooperation on my part will speed things up!"

Little Billy had attended Sunday school long enough to realize that faith is *doing*. Perhaps he remembered that St. James pointed out that faith without works is lifeless.

"I WANT FAITH . . ."

A woman in her fifties approached her pastor after hearing a sermon on the power of faith to change things. "I would like to know how to put my faith to work," she frankly stated.

"First tell me exactly where you wish to apply it," he requested. "What is your specific desire? What do you wish to change for the better?"

She shyly hesitated. "Please don't laugh, but I want faith to believe that my telephone will ring. You see," she hastened to explain, "it gets pretty dreary living alone. Things would be much better if a cheery voice called me up now and then."

"I think that's a perfectly wonderful idea," her pastor agreed. "What have you done about it?"

She shrugged. "I've tried to have faith that it will happen. But it never does."

"Tell me, Mrs. Blake, do you ever make calls yourself?"

"Not very often."

"Why not?"

"Pastor," she painfully explained, "it's like this. I feel that if I make the first calls that others will return them out of sheer duty. And I wouldn't like that. I want spontaneous voices, I want to be surprised, I want others to seek me out."

"So do they."

"What?"

"They're possibly sitting there right now waiting for your surprise call. If you will pardon my bluntness, Mrs. Blake, you have no faith at all that others will ring you up. You are talking and acting in the very way that disconnects you from cheery voices."

"What do you mean?"

"Just this. If you really had faith in a busy telephone you would get busy yourself. Let me suggest that you think of faith as your finger."

"As my finger?"

USE YOUR FINGER-FAITH

"Yes. Put that faithful finger into the dial the minute you get home. Deliberately call someone. Talk about the weather. Ask her if she likes cherry pie. Put an active faith in your own calls and you will never again worry about that silent telephone."

A week later she dialed her pastor. "Surprise!" she chuckled. "I just want to tell you that I've had six calls in the last two days."

"So you now have faith that cheery voices are seeking you out?"

"Yes!"

"What proves your faith?"

"*My* calls and *their* calls!" She beamed as she held up her forefinger. "If I can do all this with just my finger-faith, just think what will happen when I use everything else!"

SHOW YOUR FAITH BY YOUR WORKS

You see, *doing* is *having*. Can you *have* money without first doing something to earn it? Can you *have* a home without that home first being constructed? Likewise, can you have the profits of your faith without first doing something with your faith? Put it this way: Faith is *performance* toward the thing in which one has faith. The *performance* of your faith—*even though at first performed in doubt and weakness*—eventually produces the *object* of your faith.

You can never enjoy anything that is experimentally foreign to yourself. You must be an abiding citizen of a country in order to participate in its full privileges. Likewise, only when you know faith by active citizenship can you benefit from its privileges.

Prove your declared faith by living out what you declare!

Take this as your daily motto: "I will show . . . my faith by my works." (James 2:18).

DEVELOP YOUR HIDDEN PERSONALITY POWERS

Have your ever heard of psychodrama? Dr. J. L. Moreno is a pioneer and promoter of this widely used psychological technique which develops personality powers through the use of stage dramatics. It has proven highly effective when used by both children and adults. For example, a shy person is assigned the dramatic role of a bold hero such as Richard the Lion-Hearted. The shyness soon disappears as the assumed role is absorbed into the very character of the actor. By speaking and acting the bold role he actually takes on the bold characteristics of the person he represents. After a while it is no longer an assumed role, it is a permanent and very real part of the person's personality. It is an astonishingly helpful method for building faith in one's self.

You can also use this technique for generating a practical faith which will turn hoped-for characteristics into present powers.

HOW TO BECOME A STAR PERFORMER IN YOUR LIFE-DRAMA

1. Select your desired role—one that portrays confidence, patience, triumph, or whatever.
2. Forget who you are. Concentrate only upon the triumphant person you are becoming.
3. Act out your role by every means possible; in speech, thoughts, attitudes, physical movements.
4. Act it out wherever you are; in the home, at work, when you are alone and when you are with others.
5. Speak only from your positive script.
6. Bear in mind that *there is absolutely nothing to prevent you from becoming that triumphant performer*. Perhaps your former self was limited by fear or discouragement but *you are now playing a new part that has no such restrictions*. It is impossible for Richard the Lion-Hearted to be Richard the Lion-Hearted and be faint-hearted at the same time. You are not you, you are Richard the Lion-Hearted.
7. If you flub a line, forget it. What professional performer would toss away a starring role just because he now and then misses his cue?
8. Encourage yourself with the thought that you have a friendly and appreciative audience which is eager to applaud your new role.
9. Review your daily performance. Find out just where your script might be improved. Now write it into your next appearance.

I recall a man who selected *creative energy* as his desired characteristic. Writing down a list of great men who achieved notable things with creative energy he reminded himself, "In this situation I have the daring of Washington . . . I now speak with the courage of Winston Churchill . . . my attitude toward this challenge is similar in poise to that of Lincoln . . . I act with the strength of a Samson."

By thus concentrating on shining examples, he gradually released the creative energies that were residing within himself (just as you also have unreleased creativeness). In an astounding way he then used them in his own way for his own successes.

SEE YOURSELF IN AN IDEAL ROLE—AND YOU'LL BE WHAT YOU SEE

A young dramatic student asked a noted actress the secret of her ability to play the role of Joan of Arc so realistically.

To the student's surprise the actress replied, "I never play the role of St. Joan."

"But I saw you last night," insisted the student.

"You didn't see me," the actress explained, "you saw Joan of Arc. I was *Joan of Arc.*"

"Yes," the student agreed, "you were. Not once did I see you; all I saw was St. Joan."

This is the secret we have been emphasizing throughout these pages. Here is what you need to do: Speak of yourself as the very person you want to be. Ask yourself, "How would I speak and act if I were that ideal person?" Now speak and act accordingly. After a while the role will become the person. The ideal becomes the real. Your new role will attract new and appreciative audiences.

The story is told of a young man who many years ago surrounded his life with great ideals. He saw himself as a contributor of noble things to mankind. His persistent visions turned into reality when he became world-famous as an expert in the following fields: statesman, patriot, diplomat, inventor, scientist, author, editor, publisher, philosopher, wit, businessman, postmaster-general, military strategist, educator, advisor to the President of the United States. The name of this amazing man who used his self-made prophecies as a power for fulfilling them? Benjamin Franklin.

Remember, any verbal attitude that you take—even an assumed one—has the tendency to turn itself into the real thing. It grows according to the original concept. It multiplies after its kind. So why not rightly and richly multiply yourself? Many folks do this without a full knowledge of this law of reproduction. You have the advantage of knowing what you are doing.

CONSCIOUSLY SPOKEN WORDS CREATE NEW BELIEF PATTERNS . . . AND NEW BELIEF PATTERNS CREATE A NEW YOU

Your daily behavior reveals what you believe about yourself. Nothing could be more obvious. The person who believes himself to be frustrated has no choice but to act out his frustration; the truly loving individual casually reveals his belief with loving expressions. Beliefs produce states. Says Henry David Thoreau: "What a man thinks of himself, that is which determines, or rather indicates, his fate."

To change the self you must change the deep subconscious (not the shallow and fickle conscious) belief-pictures which you hold of yourself.

Says the well-known psychologist, Dr. David Seabury: "We can will to believe in the ways of life that will set us free of any mental and emotional abnormality, and the more hope we have that the healing will come, the more surely and fully it will come. In coming it will bring more good fortune with it, for life treats us in relation to the state or condition we ourselves are in." [2]

You can change your beliefs—and thus your life conditions—by speaking the kind of words that picture a new self.

Here is how one young lady did it:

She took employment in a large industrial firm, only to find to her dismay that her job required a full measure of poise and self-confidence while dealing with fellow-employees and the public. Though quite capable of desk details she found herself

[2] David Seabury, *High Hopes for Low Spirits* (Boston: Little, Brown & Company, 1955).

tongue-tied and hesitant when handling people. She tearfully entered the office of the personnel manager to request a "safe" job.

Feeling that he could solve her personality problem and also save a valuable employee, he asked her the exact difficulty, to which she replied, "I can do everything but talk. I get rattled, upset."

"MAKE BELIEVE THAT YOU ARE..."

"I used to have the same problem," confessed her boss, "so let me tell you how I licked it. I simply made believe that I was a skilled and self-confident conversationalist and then proceeded to talk as if it were true. It wasn't long before it was as actually true as I had made believe.

"Now how about you?" he asked her. "Will you put it to the test? Will you make believe that you are a self-confident person by talking that way?"

"You mean to deliberately talk myself into a new belief in myself?"

"That's a good way to put it." He requested as she rose, "Start right now. What would you say to me if you believed that it will work?"

She got the point. "I'd tell you that it is as good as done. So . . ." she smiled, "it's as good as done!"

In due time it was done. She conditioned herself into new poise by speaking in a way that was *contrary to her self-doubting uneasiness.* For example, when a chief dispatcher touched her feelings by questioning her wisdom in allotting two trucks for a job which he thought needed only one, she politely spoke up, "My judgment calls for two. Here, scan this list of deliveries." He agreed that she was correct, but her thrill came as a realization that even if she had turned out to be in error she had not only commanded respect from the dispatcher but had added to her own self-command. In another instance she went against her timid feelings to suggest to her boss that coffee-breaks would be more enjoyable if a cabinet for cups and snacks were provided. Whenever she glanced at that new cabinet she smiled at the new reflection of herself in it!

IF YOU WILL ALSO ASSUME THAT YOU HAVE FAITH . . .

When you apply this idea of faith-assumed you will be practicing a dynamic principle of faith-in-action—the very same principle that enabled St. Paul to heal the sick, the same faith that carried Columbus to a New World, the same belief that makes millions of dollars for an industrialist and a happy home for a wife.

"According to your faith be it unto you." (Matthew 9:29)

If you will now assume that the above statement is true you will eventually arrive at that magnificent station in life where faith is no longer a word to be defined but an experience to be enjoyed.

According to your faith in these words will your life always be unto you.

Assume it to be true. Speak as if it were true. And it will be true.

AN AFFIRMATIVE ALPHABET FOR ACTIVE, ABIDING ASSURANCE

No one has ever devised a better method for learning anything than the familiar A B C's. Make faith power familiar to you with this affirmation alphabet:

A stands for **authority** which I daily exert over myself and my speech.

B stands for **blessings** which are mine to give and receive.

C means personal **courage** in every situation.

D stands for the **daring** with which I revise my life for the better.

E represents a constant flow of **energy** throughout my whole personality and physical body.

F stands for the **faith** with which I meet and overcome all challenges.

G proclaims that **God** is my ever-present Power.

H means that I maintain a spirit of **humor** and good cheer.

I means that **I** am as unlimited as I believe myself to be.

J stands for the **joy** of which I am fully capable.

K represents increasing **knowledge** which daily waters my growth.

L means **love** in my life.

M means **manifestation** of those good things I desire.

N declares my **newness** of speech habits.

O stands for abundant **opportunities** wherever I go.

P promises **peace** of mind.

Q means my **quickness** in correctly responding with positive words and deeds.

R stands for my **riches** of all that life freely offers.

S means certain **security** in all phases of my life.

T represents **tenderness** in all my human relations.

U proclaims those **unusual** and refreshing feelings that are becoming more usual to me every day.

V assures me of giant-size **vitality.**

W means that I am a **winner.**

X represents the present **excellence** of my rate of increase.

Y means I **yield** myself only to positive speech.

Z stands for the **zeal** with which I affirm this entire affirmation alphabet!

SEE THE END . . . FIRST!

Have you ever tuned in your television set to find yourself viewing the final moments of a drama? Out of curiosity you might have watched it long enough to see the hero win the girl or the cowboy capture the bandit. It satisfied you, didn't it? even though you had no idea of the challenges the heroes had to overcome. The happy ending gave you a fine feeling of satisfaction and fulfillment.

Let me give you another fine idea for releasing your own heroic characteristics so that you may also end your daily dramas in an equally satisfying manner.

1. Whenever you have a problem to solve or a goal to attain, forget the obstacles that seem to be in the way. The cowboy had his bandits and Indians; you have circumstances and confusion as your challenges. But forget them as best you can: think only of the happy ending. Relax in an easy chair and pretend that you are watching the final reel. Imaginatively see things turning out in just the way that would leave you fully content. Deliberately force a smile, try to induce a feeling of fulfillment as you see yourself accomplishing your goal.

2. Verbally express your satisfaction. Happily remark, "Well, what do you know. I made it! How foolish of me to spend all that time worrying about a happy ending. I should have known better." Add other word-power encouragements as they occur to you.

3. Now perform any practical task that will actually further that completion. If it's a better job you want, look around for it. If it's a desirable character trait, start practicing it. Do anything, for, "The great man is the man who does a thing for the first time."

4. As you take your practical steps, constantly remember that you are in the final reel of your drama. Refuse to fight the bandits and Indians of the first reel. Repeat your signs of satisfaction. See only the happy ending . . . and sooner or later you will experience it. Work backward and you will carry yourself forward.

"FAITH HAS A POWER ALL ITS OWN"

A woman with sincere ambitions for becoming a published author once told me that she was about to give up hope of ever having her book published. She was disheartened at the lack of results in spite of all her efforts. I supplied her with the above pointers which she promptly put into action by doing the following: She made a book jacket out of wrapping paper and wrote on it the name of her book with her own name as author, then used it as a jacket for one of her reference books. Every morning before commencing work she gratefully looked at it while enthusiastically declaring, "My book! It's published!" This self-induced emotional lift gave her extra energies for seeking out and adding sparkling material to her manuscript. She eventually exclaimed to me, "My book! It's published! Really!" She thoughtfully added, "Faith has a power all its own."

BELIEVE THESE POINTERS FROM CHAPTER 5

1. Understand that your faith-level is always equal with the way you live, with what you do, with what you say.

2. Start walking toward your goal with what little faith you have, even with none at all. You will surely generate the faith power to reach it.

3. Where you now are is the perfect place for you to now start walking!

4. For pure power, declare your faith in yourself with pure, positive language. Know that saying is believing.

5. Close your ears to the opinion of your fickle emotions and the negative remarks of others! Hear only your declarations of faith!

6. Relax and rejoice in the truth, "A faithful man shall abound with blessings."

7. Uplift your belief in yourself by insisting upon speech patterns that insist upon your new concept of yourself.

8. Realize that an assumed faith will result in the real thing.

9. Affirm and practice your faith-building A B C's.

10. Picture only the end. See your challenges as solved or your goal as already attained.

TO RAISE YOURSELF: PRAISE YOURSELF!

Chapter 6

LIKE YOURSELF! ENJOY YOURSELF! Accept the fact that you are a winner! Dare to say nice things about yourself!

Volunteer self-praise. Freely accept praise from others. Never accept any ideas of inadequacy. Never believe that a compliment is undeserving. Allow praise to serve you . . . you *deserve* it.

And freely praise others as you would be praised . . .

PRAISING POWER IS RAISING POWER

When you have mastered the technique of using praise power you will have a joy-giving tool that will energize your abilities in every circumstance or problem. You will discover the potent truth that you are *not* a prisoner behind tightly locked doors. You will discover with both amazement and gratitude that you are truly a master locksmith with every freedom-key at your command.

THE OBJECT OF USING PRAISE POWER

Author Kenneth Hildebrand writes: "To reach our highest potential we must begin *by accepting ourselves as we are* and not as someone expects or desires us to be." [1]

[1] Kenneth Hildebrand, *Achieving Real Happiness* (New York: Harper and Brothers, 1955).

The object of praise-acceptance is simply and only . . . *full self-acceptance.* Most folks are unaware of the startling degree to which they wastefully indulge in self-rejection. But full self-approval always results in full release of your powers and talents for achievement. Thoreau's wisdom is well worth repeating here: "What a man thinks of himself, that is which determines, or rather indicates, his fate."

Whatever you do, don't miss out on this splendid idea. It is so important that I want to devote the entire chapter to showing you exactly how to go about it. Remember—all praise is good . . . and good for you. So . . . praise yourself and raise yourself!

PRAISE YOUR ABILITIES—AND WATCH THEM GROW

You should praise your present abilities for two good reasons—because you deserve it and because it is the *sure-fire way to increase them.*

Scientific experiments with both children and adults prove that praise promotes enthusiasm, accuracy, and performance in general, while scolding, blaming, and unjust criticism destroy the creative power of the individual. Here is a conclusion drawn from one of these experiments: "The most effective incentive is shown here to be praise, which results in consistent improvement." [2]

Don't *you* glow when praised, even in a small way? Doesn't it make *you* want to do bigger and better things? Every time! Remember this as you proceed with the chapter.

I repeat, you can awaken your present abilities simply by praising them at every opportunity. Take my word for it. Better yet, take your own praise-full words for it and prove it for yourself.

[2] Edwin Garrigues Boring, Herbert Sidney Langfeld, Harry Porter Weld, eds., *Foundations of Psychology* (New York: John Wiley & Sons, Inc., 1948).

IT WORKS! . . . IT WORKS FOR YOU!

Let me tell you how one man opened himself to a refreshing inflow of personality power.

He said, "At the front of my house there are fifteen steps leading from the lower sidewalk to my elevated front yard. With just these fifteen little brick steps I developed a system for instilling myself with a whole new personality. Those fantastic fifteen steps!

"In my mind's eye I assigned each step the name of a characteristic that I wanted to add to my personality. I started with some of the traits that were already a part of me but which I wished to increase. Thus, the lower steps were assigned such traits as persistence, enthusiasm, hope. The upper steps represented those traits which were a lesser part of me, such as confidence, relaxation, clarity of purpose.

"During the course of the day I naturally ascended the steps several times. Each time I informed myself that I was climbing up to those desirable qualities. I told myself, 'You are advancing upward with persistence, enthusiasm, cheeriness, relaxation. Every time you take an upward step you are bit-by-bit absorbing these fine features into yourself. Every step takes you nearer and nearer the top where a whole new personality awaits you. Just keep stepping up . . . up . . . up . . . that's all you have to do.' "

He finished his success story by happily telling me, "As strange as it seems, those cold, impersonal steps in my front yard turned into warm, personal characteristics in my personality. I became a new man down at the office and in my home. Just ask my wife!"

These very real improvements came about as a result of his *expanded self-picture. As he firmly viewed himself as he wanted to be, he released and directed his inner creative powers—which turned the pictured self into a real self.*

IF THIS SOUNDS UNUSUAL TO YOU . . .

If this technique—or any other method suggested in this book—seems unusual to you, you will read in Chapter 8 of some happy folks who dared to do the unfamiliar. Their unusual procedures brought about unusual—and highly welcomed—results. So refuse to be tied down by traditional means . . . for it means so much to you.

TAKE DOWN-TO-EARTH STEPS WHILE KEEPING THE HEAVENLY VISION

If you want poetry in your life, first be practical. After a while you will be practically poetic.

I now want to give you an exact procedure for using your praise power for stepping up to the pinnacles where all of life's riches are freely yours.

1. WHAT CAN YOU DO RIGHT NOW?

Think of something that you easily accomplish right now. It can be *anything,* no matter how large or small. Just think for a moment and come up with any little task that you presently perform with confidence and success. Do you consider yourself a careful and considerate driver? Can you reupholster a chair better than most? Can you trim a tree or train a parrot or recite the alphabet backward without making a mistake? Get something, anything, for *everyone* can do *something* very well.

2. YOU CAN DO IT . . . SO PRAISE IT!

Got it! Fine! Now *praise* it. Say to yourself, "Unaccustomed as I am to private praise, I now have something nice to say about myself: 'I can identify every bird that flits into my backyard' " (or whatever your particular talent may be). Now continue your self-praise with something like, "Yes, sir, I know the name of every winged creature I see. I'll bet there isn't another person in the whole community who can do this. I'm unique!"

(Incidentally, there's no harm in doing this in a light, casual manner, just as long as you really mean business. You'll get the serious point in a minute.)

State all the honest facts you can dig up concerning your achievement (for they *are* facts, you know). Let yourself know that you are the finest or the most accurate or the fastest or the most painstaking. You've already got it, so give it everything you've got. (Forget modesty for the moment, we'll come to that later.)

3. SELECT THAT NEW GOAL

Next, think of something that you would like to do (or a personality trait you'd like to add) but which is not a present part of your achievements. Got it? Now declare your ability to achieve it in the same excellent, efficient manner as that previous accomplishment of yours. Associate the two. Tie them together. Make them one. Consider them identical twins. State these exact words: "Since I have achieved *this,* I can also achieve *that!*" Repeat it several times. The idea is to join your past success with your present goal. Compliment yourself that the one will have as equally successful an outcome as the other. Praise the past successful task, praise the present new task, praise yourself for your effort.

4. GET GOING

Now get going on that new goal. Start doing it. Start *anywhere.* You must start somewhere, so start *anywhere,* even if it seems haphazard. Just plain start. As you proceed, affirm your powers, praise your progress, repeat over and over, "Since I achieved *this,* I can also achieve *that.*" Drive yourself into the understanding that there is really no difference in the two—the identical twins are also identical in success. Believe that if you are successful *here,* you are also successful *there.* As you continue to do this you will see that it is not the geography that counts, but rather the world traveler who can go anywhere and do anything.

5. YOU SEE! YOU DID IT!

If you have proceeded thus far, your goal is now more than merely in sight. Your feet are actually planted on that higher ground right now. Now strengthen your footing by actually standing on the first step of a flight of steps. Now easily, casually, walk halfway up the flight. Halt. Stand still for a moment and look down at the steps you have just climbed. Declare, "See, I have actually made progress!"

Now look upward to the very top step and repeat, "If I can stand *here,* I can also stand *there.*" Now as easily and casually as before, step up to the very top. Look around at the fine view. Relax your muscles, let them droop. Take a deep breath. Smile. Confidently remark to yourself, "I *said* I could do it, I *knew* I could do it—and I *did* it!"

Now do you see how praising power can be practically applied as raising power? Every word of praise releases your inner confidences, expands your faith. You gain a new insight that reveals *no* obstacles on either your psychological steps or the stone ones. You impress yourself with the confidence that you can step upward just as easily as you can . . . step upward. Psychologist Matthew N. Chappell advises: "Properly used, speech, talk, and recitation are valuable psychological assets. Use them to attain the ends you seek, not those you seek to avoid." [3]

Do you have some steps handy? Use them for stepping up to life!

ENERGIZE YOURSELF WITH VOCAL VITAMINS

Every energetic word you speak is a vocal vitamin. So use it as such. Whenever you need a lift or a smile or a refreshment, treat yourself to your verbal vitamins. Include a vitamin of valiancy, a mineral of modesty, a calorie of confidence. You will

[3] Matthew N. Chappell, *In the Name of Common Sense* (rev. ed.; New York: Macmillan Company, 1955). Quotation used with permission of the Macmillan Company.

grow and glow; people who look your way will see a healthy loveliness about you.

WHAT ONE WOMAN DISCOVERED

A lady living in Des Moines relates:

I'll never forget that Wednesday afternoon. It was one of the happiest—and funniest—things that ever happened to me. It was the day I discovered that everyone else had a better opinion of me than I had of myself. Me, the girl who thought she might be somewhat on the vain side, held herself in far less esteem than her husband, her children, her friends. It was a startling revelation that changed my life!

It all started during an afternoon lull when Mary, my friend and neighbor, dropped in for coffee and chatter. Mary was the neighborhood cut-up who was currently on a personality-improvement binge.

"It says here," Mary explained as she opened a magazine on the kitchen table, "that you can increase your self-confidence and make yourself generally happier simply by changing the way you speak!"

"Oh?" I absently stirred my coffee, wondering if Tommy would remember to get his repaired shoes on the way home from school.

She took a pencil off the window ledge. "Let's test it. Here's the first question: *What kind of a cook are you?*"

I shrugged. "Oh, fairly good . . . sometimes."

"Ah!" Mary tapped the magazine. "See!"

"See what?" I asked, my curiosity rising.

"The honest fact is—you are not a *sometimes fair* cook. You are a *good* cook."

I laughed. "I am?"

"Of *course* you are. For one thing, I've seen that husband of yours in action at the dinner table. You have no business ever referring to yourself in any other way but as a *good cook*. And since you *are* a good cook you can *call* yourself a good cook and *feel* like a good cook."

"I-am-a-good-cook," I mechanically repeated with a smile.

Mary squinted at the page. "According to this chart you should feel at least 3 per cent better. How about it?"

SELF-ACCEPTANCE INDUCES A NEW FEELING—A JUSTIFIED FEELING

"Maybe it sounds silly, but I *do* feel better. *Really.*" I meant it, although I wasn't quite sure what was happening.

She made a check mark. "Okay. Now we get into your personality: *Are you a pleasant person?*"

"Uh . . . sometimes I get angry."

"That has nothing to do with it," she emphatically replied.

"What do you mean? It seems to have *everything* to do with it."

RESPOND **CORRECTLY**

"It's the way you respond to the question," she said. "Of course you sometimes get angry. So does everyone else. Even people who are very pleasant."

"I don't get it," I said, "how *should* I have answered the question?"

"You should have replied, *Yes, I am very pleasant. I may make occasional human mistakes in my dealings with others but I am really a nice person.* You see," she jabbed at the book, "an occasional mistake does not make you an unpleasant person any more than falling in the lake makes a chicken a duck. A chicken may momentarily *act* like a duck, but that doesn't *make* him one."

I had to laugh outright at that one. "I get it! I have no business concentrating on an occasional slip-up when judging myself."

"You are a pleasant person almost all the time. It's the majority that rules.

"I-am-a-pleasant-person," I solemnly intoned and we both smiled.

"It says here," Mary read from the magazine, "that our use of words doesn't exactly change the situation in these particular cases, but it does change our viewpoint toward them."

IT'S YOUR ATTITUDE THAT COUNTS—YOUR WORDS CHANGE YOUR VIEWPOINT

"In other words, it's the attitude that counts."

"Right! Let's try one more."

I held up crossed fingers. "Ready!"

"Do you like yourself?"

"Well . . ." I hesitated, "I guess so. But I have plenty of faults."

"There you go again! . . . Plenty of faults."

I laughed and threw up my arms. "What in the wide world is a better answer?"

Mary searched the column: *"There are lots of nice things about me."*

"Of course there are lots of nice things about me, but . . ."

"But *nothing*," she interrupted. "There are lots of nice things about you, so you can honestly claim, *I like myself.*"

"Well, I'll be . . ." I gasped. "Now that you put it *that* way . . ."

WHEN YOU **SAY** LIFE IS BETTER—YOU MAKE IT SO

"Life is better simply because you *say* so," she finished. "Now according to the article you should feel at least 10 per cent better."

"At least 50 per cent," I agreed, and it was true, I *did* feel better. Right then and there I realized I had discovered something of prime importance to my sense of well-being. I knew that from that day forward I would never indulge in needless self-devaluation that had so often led to moodiness. Instead, I would harmonize friend-praise with self-praise. Two *saids* were better than one! It has never ceased to give me a sound psychological lift.

TRUE MODESTY IS A DESSERT—SERVE YOURSELF

"All right," a reader may admit at this point, "I'm sold on the idea. Praise power is everything you say. But wait a minute. Something bothers me. My mental habit-system is objecting. It whispers, 'What's this? Agree with praise and appreciation? Even serve it to myself? Just like that? . . . frankly and calmly? What will people think? Won't they wonder at the size of my head?' "

No, they won't, not when you do it properly. As a matter of fact they will begin to wonder at the size of your personality. Let me illustrate this for you.

Imagine yourself in a fashionable—and a bit unusual—cafe. It serves *personality* instead of food. You look over the menu and tell the waiter, "Please serve me with a generous portion of that delicious dish you call True Modesty. I am eager to enjoy it."

"Yes," replies the waiter, "but you must first enjoy our preliminary dishes of Confidence and Achievement."

"All right," you agree, "please first serve me with Confidence and Achievement."

As soon as you finish those two dishes the waiter cheerfully appears with a heaping portion of True Modesty. "See," he points out, "this is the correct sequence of dishes. Now that you have had your Confidence and Achievement you are ready for True Modesty."

"Right!" you exclaim, "True Modesty is always a dessert!"

MODESTY, SELF-ASSURANCE, AND SELF-ACHIEVEMENT ARE THREE-IN-ONE

We find no self-depreciation or false modesty in the great men and women of history who have contributed noteworthy things to mankind. Joseph of Egypt, the apostle Paul, Washington, Lincoln, Winston Churchill and all the rest have proved that self-assurance, self-achievement and self-modesty are actually three-in-one.

MAKE THIS CLEAR IN YOUR THINKING

Vanity is a fault, not because the vain person thinks well of himself, but because he really doesn't. The vain person hopes he has found himself, the modest person knows that he has. Vanity says, "If I am noticed I will feel attractive"; self-confidence says, "I will be noticed because I am attractive."

Remember the four vital *V*'s:

VALID VIRTUE VANQUISHES VANITY

You can always modestly adapt praise power to any situation. Instead of sounding vain you will sound like a man who knows where he stands with himself and with others . . . and it is others who will then mark you as a truly modest person.

A Methodist minister who richly deserves commendation for his fine sermons usually says something like, "Thank you. I appreciate hearing that my studies are worth while."

A Los Angeles housewife was heard to chuckle when her new hair-do received attention, "I adore it! Who *wouldn't* adore something that took all day!"

A college football hero had the right idea when he admitted, "I *did* race through that line, didn't I? But thanks to the rest of the squad."

DISCOVER YOURSELF—GIVE YOURSELF CREDIT

There is no more noble task than seeking about to discover yourself, to gain a true appraisal, to find that you are a much nicer person than you give yourself credit for.

Know this:

OTHERS SEE YOU AS YOU FIRST SEE YOURSELF

Do you know that others see you as you first see yourself? Their evaluation of you is based on the way you speak and act—and you always speak and act in the way you *believe yourself to be.* Psychology calls this a form of projection, that is, we project out own attitudes, we believe that others think the same thoughts we think, we believe them to be as we are. Therefore, if you believe yourself to be unworthy you will also attribute unworthy beliefs toward others—and there goes your acceptance by others. With that insight so characteristic of great poets, John Greenleaf Whittier of Massachusetts wrote of this business of "judging others by ourselves":

> **"Search thine own heart. What paineth thee in others in thyself may be."**

The solution is wonderfully clear. If you want others to accept you, you must first accept yourself. And then, to paraphrase Whittier: "What delighteth thee in thyself, will others also delight in."

This self-help idea alone should cause you to shout in praise!

WHY SELF-ACCEPTANCE IS SO VITAL IN YOUR LIFE

Someone may chuckle at this point, "I'll let you in on a little secret. I *do* accept praise. As a matter of fact, I can't lap it up fast enough!"

But there is much more than appears on the surface. The values lie far deeper than the temporary thrill of hearing a compliment. We want those expressions of worthiness to carry far beyond the mere ecstasy of the moment. We want them to transform us, to so dominate us that we *know* beyond any shadow of doubt that we are worthy. Only then do our frantic outer searchings for inner comfort cease, and only then do we peacefully enjoy our own company for the first time.

At various times and in various circumstances we have all been verbally torpedoed. There is not a single reader of this book who has not been on the receiving end of something like:

"What makes you so careless?"

"That's *not* the way to do it!"

"How many times must I tell you?"

Incidentally, the very reading of these phrases in print may stir your emotions to some degree or other, even though you may not be fully conscious of them. You may feel vaguely uncomfortable, even resentful at their presence. Now is the time to frankly drag these emotions out into the open. And now that they are faced we are ready to counter them with positive word power. The old feelings are on their way out! We refuse them—

absolutely, flatly, once-and-for-all, for they are dishonest evaluations.

REFUSE TO ALLOW YOUR PAST TO CONTROL YOUR PRESENT

Have you ever attended a school reunion? Were you surprised at the changes in your former classmates? Let me tell you of a former classmate of mine.

I'll call him Wilbur Norwich, but to everyone in school he was better known as Flubber. Flubber flubbed everything . . . his studies, his athletics, his social affairs. A nice boy, you understand, but one of those poor souls who miserably fouled up everything he touched.

On the day of the picnic reunion, up walked Flubber. But to everyone's amazement he was someone else. Flubber no longer looked like Flubber. Instead, he was a tall, keen-looking individual who wore a handsome naval officer's uniform. A captain, no less! Captain Wilbur Norwich, U.S.N.

As we sat on the picnic benches our curiosity was rewarded, for Flubber—I mean Captain Norwich—was very frank about it.

"Sure I was a flubber in school," he cheerfully admitted, "but a few months after graduation I discovered a fantastic truth which I'll sum up for you in just nine words: *My past has nothing to do with my present.*

"It took me time," he told us, "but I cut it short by telling myself over and over that the Willy Norwich of high school was *not* the Mr. Wilbur Norwich who finally graduated. Whatever I was *then,* need have nothing to do with what I wanted to be *now.*"

REFUSE TO BE DEGRADED

"The first thing I did," said the captain, "was to refuse to be verbally torpedoed any longer. I refused to believe any past or present torpedoes of failure, incompetence, ridicule, derision. During high school I had little skill in dodging their hurt, for I was young and susceptible to suggestion. Every time a torpedo-like word or experience plunged into my midsection it exploded with fearful emotional reaction, allowing torrents of self-reproach to gush in. I was so dazed by the explosion that I believed that I was exactly what others said I was—inadequate, stupid, and so on.

"But I took the stand that from this point on I was unsinkable. Verbal torpedoes no longer had any target in me. I was the captain and I'll be switched if I allow anyone in either the past or present to degrade my rank. I am in complete charge of my ship—and no one had better forget it!"

YOU ARE THE CAPTAIN

You are also the captain of your ship of life. Take charge! Stand on the deck and give orders. Forget the torpedoes. They can't touch you, for you are in command of every action. Talk and act like the present captain you are!

CHART A NEW COURSE IN LIFE

"I found," the captain's story continued, "that when I deliberately accepted only good things about myself I gradually dislodged those old torpedo fragments, those held-over false feelings. Little by little I worked them over the side. My water line rose as the weight of their burden slipped overboard. I began to sail with ease on the very top of the waves and with increasing speed. I started to sail the way I wanted to sail . . . smoothly, confidently, steadily forward. I was in my *rightful* command."

COMMAND YOURSELF—AND COMMAND LIFE'S HIGH SEAS!

Like Captain Norwich, you can take a new command of your life by simply charting a new course, by volunteering and accepting self-promotions in every way possible.

New feelings of worthiness may enter in the form of vocal praise, a compliment for a job well done, through reading the Bible, even when listening to inspiring music. Your aim is to permit penetration of all outside energizers so that they are translated into inner resources.

THREE VITAL STEPS TO SELF-ELEVATION

Know that:

Praise power gives you confidence.
Confidence gives you achievement ability.
Achievement results in true modesty.

UPLIFTING IDEAS FOR AN UPLIFTED LIFE

1. Use praise power as a means for full self-acceptance.

2. Watch your abilities grow as you praise them.

3. Practice the effective technique of associating your new goals with your present successes.

4. Speak well of yourself, think well of yourself . . . and act the way you speak and think.

5. Know that only the truly self-confident can be truly modest.

6. Constantly give full credit to yourself and to others.

7. Refuse to be degraded by anyone or anything. Quietly believe in yourself.

8. Remember that you are a capable captain.

9. Chart a new verbal and mental course. Don't drift, keep your destination in view at all times.

10. Leave yourself wide open to all compliments. Accept them as personal energizers.

HOW TO TURN YOUR SPEECH POWER INTO SUCCESS POWER

Chapter 7

"MY WHOLE SECRET OF SUCCESS," revealed the owner of a highly popular Florida resort, "is to create my desired self in imagination and repeatedly affirm that I am that very person I imagine myself to be."

This is a simple and simply fantastic way of freeing yourself from every limitation that now holds you in bondage. Regardless of how high those walls seem, you can soar over them by:

1. Imagining yourself as your desired self.
2. Sustaining your imaginative picture with positive verbal attitudes.

Dr. David Seabury has this to say about imagination: "When respected and understood, it is the means by which you can command your will to achieve what you desire." [1]

DO YOU WANT A FAITH THAT MOVES MOUNTAINS? REMEMBER—FAITH AND IMAGINATION ARE IN INTIMATE UNION

This very day you have acted either successfully or unsuccessfully because you first imaginatively pictured yourself acting that way. Perhaps you entered a restaurant because you first saw yourself as being satisfied with the results of your entry. Or you may have met defeat in solving a personal problem

[1] David Seabury, *High Hopes for Low Spirits* (Boston: Little, Brown & Company, 1955).

because your negative imagination first prophetically pictured that defeat—and you drew that defeat to yourself by believing the false prophecy.

You can easily see how you use your imagination in practically everything you do. I'd like you to carefully consider the fact that your faith is, in one sense, your imaginative pictures. You see what you believe is there. The secret of success is to picture *yourself* as you wish to *be,* and turn your back on *things* as they *are.* Doesn't this give you a richer understanding of the New Testament declaration, "For we walk by faith, not by sight."? (II Corinthians 5:7)

HERE'S HOW ONE MAN ACTUALLY CREATES THE VERY SUCCESS HE IMAGINES

A cab driver relates: "All day long as I cruise the city I imagine myself as busy every minute. I see myself hailed from every direction, I find myself carrying passengers on long trips, I imagine that every fare is going to be a well-rewarding one. No sooner do I drop one fare than another appears from nowhere.

"I encourage my imaginative success by doing everything possible to turn it into reality. Immediately upon hitting a cab phone I ask the dispatcher what's waiting for me, I cruise expectantly past after-theater patrons, I urge passengers to make their return trip with me. My combination of imaginative pictures and practical operations has a miraculous way of hardening into success.

"I don't claim to understand how or why this works, but I do know that this self-urged feeling of success gives me one of the top incomes of the cab fleet. I imagine I am one of the few drivers who uses this technique, for I have won the company top-man award three times in the last year."

YOUR IMAGINATION—LIKE YOUR SPEECH—MUST BE DOMINATED BY THE POSITIVE

Every man is always what he imagines (what he *believes*) himself to be. It is impossible to be anything else. Your actual self perfectly conforms to your pictured self. They are one, they are inseparable. Therefore, the certain way to change the actual self is to charge your imaginative speech with every possible type of positive speaking. Negative speech confirms and sustains the negative self-picture, but positive speech paints the new one that you desire.

Spinoza defines this psychological law: "So long as a man imagines that he cannot do this or that, so long is he determined not to do it: and consequently, so long it is impossible to him that he should do it."

A creative imagination is possible; therefore creation is possible.

CREATE VERBAL VISIONS EVERY DAY!

You will be enormously helped by adding a new and creation-crammed phrase to your vocabulary. That phrase is *verbal vision.* A verbal vision is the act of *imaginatively seeing yourself talking as a successful person might talk.*

Here is how to create vitalizing verbal visions:

Shortly before you are to speak in a forthcoming situation, visualize yourself as speaking and acting in the manner that represents your idea of a calm, confident, effective person.

See yourself as saying the right thing, picture yourself as replying with authority and intelligence to the comments of others, imagine that they are pleased with you, visualize yourself as highly gratified with the total outcome.

Now enter the situation with every confidence that it will turn out with the same fine success that your verbal vision prophesied.

YOUR IMAGINATION IS YOUR MAGIC CARPET— CLIMB ABOARD YOUR SOARING VISIONS

If you will persistently soar above your present self with positive verbal visions you will magically transport yourself to the world of your dreams. This is true, this is absolute. When you weave your own magic carpet you will safely soar above every earthly problem.

Let me tell you a story of how one woman switched herself from a minus quantity to a plus-personality through the powers of her imaginative speech. She relates:

"I was a member of our large community woman's club . . . and that's all I was, just a member. It wasn't that I had political aspirations or anything like that, it was just that I wanted to enjoy myself more by taking a personal part in the various activities.

"I especially wanted to take charge of the forthcoming annual flower show. Flowers had been my eager hobby all my life and I was itching to plunge myself into a leading role. But feelings of inferiority and fear of failure held me back from volunteering for the chairmanship. In my imagination I pictured myself as failing, I heard critical remarks, I imagined everyone as displeased with my efforts. I hated myself almost to the point of withdrawing my membership, for—to put it bluntly—I was sick and tired of seeing myself as that fearful, inadequate person.

IMAGINE THAT!

"One afternoon, about a month before the exhibit, we were fortunate enough to line up a well-known lecturer whose topic was the use-and-abuse of word power. I'll never forget the first words he spoke for they turned me from a timid, miserable club member to a happy, buoyant emotionally free leader. He stepped forward on the platform and remarked:

" 'Imagine *that!*' He paused, smiled, and quietly repeated, '*Imagine* that!'

IMAGINATIVE SPEECH WORKS WONDERS

"I sat in total fascination as he developed his theme of imaginative speech: 'Imagine yourself as another person . . . talk like that other person talks . . . try to feel yourself in a new role . . . speak the way you would like to be . . . imaginative speech works wonders of personality transformation . . . *if anyone else can do it, you can do it!*'

"His last phrase struck me like a meteor on the roof. '*If anyone else can do it, you can do it.*'

"Even as he talked I started putting myself into the role of our able, confident president, Ruth Drexler. It immediately gave me new confidence to mentally tell myself that if *she* could do it, *I* could do it.

OF COURSE YOU CAN!

"A strange feeling of joy coursed through me. It was almost as if an inner self replied, 'Of *course* you can. If *she* can do it, *you* can do it.'

"During the next several days I diligently practiced imaginative speech. I imagined myself as calmly and efficiently managing the flower show, I heard myself giving suggestions to my fellow members for displaying their exhibits, I even told Ruth Drexler that her display would look better in a taller vase. I ended each session with the verbal vision of everyone congratulating me on the finest, most successful flower show ever presented.

"Do you know what happened? *Everything I had imagined!* And much more had happened to *me* as I left the auditorium. I was a totally different person than the one of a few weeks previous. Both my delight and my self-confidence knew no bounds!"

IMAGINATIVE SPEECH IS YOUR LADDER—CLIMB IT DAILY

Since the whole secret of personality transformation (and thus *circumstance transformation*) lies in the faculty of first seeing yourself as a new person, you must use your imagination, you must use your imaginative speech. Your eyes and ears can only declare you to be what you presently see yourself as being, but new verbal conceptions free you from these limiting views. You double your assurance of escape from an unwanted self when you jointly use the keys of imagination power and word power. Truly, here is faith in action!

So picture your positive phrases as steps of a ladder whereby you will climb the heights. Every time you speak as you know you should speak, imagine that you have also taken an upward step. There is little doubt that you will soon have your head in some very real clouds.

IF YOU FEEL PINNED DOWN AND TIED UP . . .

A research scientist, engaged in a vital government project, reported to his physician that he felt pinned down, tied up, unable to fully release his creative forces.

"Here I am," he lamented, "a man with an excellent education and loads of experience. But I just don't seem to have that mental freedom or the expansive outlook that my job requires. I've *always* felt that way. Can anything be done about it?"

The physician questioned him long enough to discover that his ability to see himself as a free, uninhibited person had somehow been lost along the way; consequently he had no way of seeing himself except as he presently was—a chained man. The solution, of course, was for him to change the picture of himself to that of a freely flowing, creative individual.

The doctor asked him to do an unusual thing. "The next time you call will you please bring me a couple of pictures of yourself?"

"You mean photographs?"

"Yes. One of yourself as a boy and a recent one."

When the scientist complied the doctor asked him to set them side by side on the desk. The doctor then asked, "Do you see much resemblance in the two?"

"Not much," the scientist admitted.

"Why not?"

"Well . . ." he studied the pictures, "I've changed . . . changed a whole lot."

"You mean your physical body is different? . . . you're taller, stronger, more fully developed?"

"That's right."

"It's difficult imagining yourself as a boy again, isn't it?"

"Almost impossible."

IT IS TRUE . . . SO GIVE THANKS

The physician held up a finger to emphasize his next words. "I want you to go home and set the pictures alongside each other. Place them where you will see them several times a day. Every time you look at them I want you to declare to yourself that your mental powers are as expanded, as grown-up, as strong as your physical body. Drill the fact into yourself that you are no longer limited by anything in your past life. You are free from everything that bothers and binds you. Look at the adult picture and declare that *everything* about you is different; not only your physical body but your thinking patterns, your emotional responses, your attitudes toward your daily efforts. Then look at this new imaginative picture and give thanks that it is true, for new imaginings will surely make it true."

The scientist got the idea. "You're telling me that I must free myself from thinking in terms of my past."

"If you do this," the doctor confirmed, "you will soon find it as impossible to be an undeveloped thinker as it is impossible for you to be an undeveloped adult. You will be as free as you imagine yourself to be."

The results were exactly as the physician had predicted. The scientist gratefully reported, "Mental and emotional freedom became so real to me that I tore up that boyhood photograph. It was a bad picture anyway."

He now pursues his scientific projects with talent, enthusiasm . . . and imagination.

The scientific basis for his attainment is found in this exciting sentence from Dr. David Seabury: "The miracles made possible when imagination is controlled by constructive attitudes leave one breathless because of their grandeur."[2]

ENLARGE YOUR TALENTS BY SPEAKING A NEW LANGUAGE

Perhaps you also have talents and abilities that yearn for free expression. If so, resolve to speak as a free man would speak.

[2] David Seabury, *High Hopes for Low Spirits* (Boston: Little, Brown & Company, 1955).

Fill your heart and tongue with imaginative words that build strong and giantlike characteristics. You will not only have giantlike strength for self-expression but you will be gloriously free from those pygmylike annoyances that divert and waste your energies.

There once lived a very tiny pygmy who was deeply displeased with his pygmylike nature. He wanted to be a giant with a giantlike nature. So he planted himself between the legs of a huge giant, cupped his hands and yelled up.

"Mr. Giant, what's your secret for growing so tall?"

"It's no secret," the giant bellowed down, "just learn to speak a new language."

"*What* new language?" asked the pygmy. "The *Spanish* language?"

"No!" roared the giant.

"It is *French?*"

"No!"

"*Chinese?*"

"No!"

"Then what language *is* it that I must speak to become a giant?"

"The *only* language a giant *can* speak," was the reply, "*Giant* language. When you *know* Giant, you *grow* giant."

So the pygmy promptly forgot all his pygmylike words and started to speak a new language which consisted of such giantlike words as *courage, persistence, faith, love.*

And every time he opened his mouth he grew an inch. The more he talked the more he grew. Before long he was a tall giant himself.

"Now that I am a big giant," he happily shouted, "I can't see those pygmylike characteristics any more."

"Of course not," said his giant friend, "you outgrew them."

WHEN YOU UNDERSTAND **THIS**, YOU WILL NEVER AGAIN BE DOWNHEARTED OR DISCOURAGED!

A few days after getting started on imaginative speech, an acquaintance droopily reported, "I try and try to see myself as a new person but it doesn't seem to work. What's the matter?"

I surprised him by replying, "Excellent! I'm glad to hear it."

"I don't understand."

"You are still seeing yourself as your *old* self, aren't you?"

"Yes."

"You have yet to get that first glimmer of yourself as that *new* person?"

"Yes."

"Do you agree that you can only see yourself as one person at a time? I mean, you can't see yourself as the old and the new simultaneously."

"Not very well."

"So you can now understand that if you are capable of seeing that present unwanted personality you are also capable of eventually seeing the wanted one. It's a question of time and persistence. Believe me, if you just keep going you will come back here and tell me that all sorts of good things are happening to you."

WHAT A TRUTH!

If *you* ever get discouraged and feel like giving up, remember:

It is only because you are still seeing yourself as you presently are, not as you wish to be.

It *is* a fact that you can only see yourself as one person at a time, but if you are capable of seeing yourself as that old person *you are also capable of eventually seeing yourself as that new one.* So consider your very discouragement as a flash of insight by emphatically declaring, "If I can be *this,* I can also be *that!*" For it is the truth.

Let's briefly repeat this thought for clarity's sake: Just as you now imagine yourself in a sorry state, unable to see the new, the time must also come when you will be unable to see the old. Just as a mature adult is unable to duplicate his previous childish ways, you will no longer be able to duplicate your former ineffective ways.

You will find it just as imposssible to be weak as you may now find it impossible to be strong! Weakness will be altogether out of your hands, just as power is now in them!

Imaginative speech is the means by which you bit-by-bit block out your former self-picture and flash before your eyes the new work of living art with all its fresh and appealing life-colors.

CREATE VITALIZING VERBAL VISIONS—DON'T JUST DAY-DREAM

"A *say*-dream is the verbal equivalent of a *day*-dream," I once told an inquirer. "Be sure that you avoid both."

He later reported, "I now see that the difference between my positive verbal visions and my verbal day-dreams is the difference between my success and failure."

A verbal vision is the bold and consistent act of creating a new image of yourself through positive speech. It means a stout refusal to speak a language that does not harmonize with your ideal. It means closing your eyes and ears to the world and opening your heart to those inner stirrings of life. It means a verbal and mental acceptance of all those good things which you desire.

Mere day-dreams vanish with the sunset, but faithful verbal visions make each sunrise a lovely one. Sustained faith in your ideal will awaken you with the sure knowledge that the day is yours to enjoy as you will.

PROVE IT YOURSELF!

The power of imagination—and imaginative speech—is not some vague, unproven principle but rather a usable, practical law that is thoroughly backed up by science, psychology, philosophy, religion . . . and common sense. If it proved true to just one man in the world it would be true, but it is proved every day by successful men and women all over the world.

Those who have known and used the overwhelming power of imaginative visions to create powerful personalities are the very ones who are known to us today:

Albert Einstein declared that imagination is even more important than knowledge.

Shakespeare wrote, "Sweeten my imagination."

The Bible declares, "Where there is no vision, the people perish." (Proverbs 29:18)

Poet John Keats sang, "I am certain of nothing but the holiness of the heart's affections, and the truth of Imagination. What the Imagination seizes as Beauty must be the Truth."

Emerson observed that we build our real world of beauty by first surrounding our lives with imaginative beauty.

IMPRESS YOURSELF WITH SUCCESS AND SUCCESS WILL EXPRESS ITSELF TO YOU

Everyone wants to make a successful impression in his own particular world. If you have been struggling unsuccessfully it is possible that you have not understood that the only way to create that successful outer expression is to first create that successful inner impression.

YOUR SUCCESS IS SIMPLY YOU . . . AND NOTHING ELSE

I'd like you to slowly read and reread this tremendous truth, for its understanding and application will give you that superior insight that you need:

Success is—first of all—*you.* It is not a circumstance or thing or position or place. Success is always only what you make it. You never create success in some mysterious or lucky manner: you are successful because *you* are successful. There can be neither success nor failure, there must be a successful or failing individual. Everything starts with you, therefore it is you that must first be transformed, not that circumstance or thing. When *you* change, circumstances change with you.

TURN YOUR IMAGINATION LOOSE **ANYWHERE** AND IT WILL LEAD YOU **SOMEWHERE**

If you have any trouble at all in getting down to business, let me give you an encouraging illustration of how one man turned his imagination loose.

An author friend of mine told me that it used to be one great chore getting started with his daily manuscripts. He said, "I'd stall around, drink coffee, fiddle with mail, do everything except start clicking those typewriter keys. My imagination was a total blank.

"One morning I made up my mind that I'd had enough; my fiddling was costing entirely too much. So I gave myself a pep-talk: 'Now look here, you claim to be a successful writer but you're just one big bundle of excuses. I want you to sit down at that typewriter and imagine yourself as a successful writer. Forget everything but your goal—a well-written story.'

"So I assumed the frame of mind that would be mine if I were actually turning out a highly readable story and started pounding out copy. And what copy! I found myself the author of this magnificent poem:

> Well-trained bears
> Don't sit in chairs,
> Instead, they find a cave;
> But if I were a bear
> I'd perch on a chair,
> And listen to everyone rave!

But to my astonishment I found that this bit of humorous verse loosened my mind and started a flow of creative ideas. One good idea led to another until I had a complete story outline in less than ten minutes!"

SPECIFIC SUCCESS LEADS TO GENERAL SUCCESS

A young businessman once called to thank me for showing him how to talk his way out of fearful, inhibited actions on the job. When I congratulated him he wrinkled his forehead and said, "But Mr. Howard, there is something happily mysterious about it. Perhaps you can solve it for me."

"What is the happy mystery?" I asked.

"As soon as I conquered my stilted work habits I began to feel much better about *everything* else," he replied. "I mean, I am much more successful in other things unconnected with my job. I don't worry so much about world affairs, I calmly handle domestic problems, I'm just at peace *all over.* How come?"

"Psychology calls it generalization," I gave the answer. "It simply means that if you are successful in one place you have the tendency to be successful in another. It's like spilling a bucket of paint in the center of the floor—it spreads all over."

If you, like the writer and the businessman, will start *anywhere,* you will soon be *somewhere.*

YOUR DAY WILL COME . . .

Are you seeking without finding? Are you knocking without entering? Are you even somewhat bitter because you feel that it is too late or too hard or too confusing?

Cheer up!

Your day will come.

And much sooner than you think!

If you faithfully practice imaginative word power you sooner or later will be at rest. You will utter a great sigh of completion, the struggle will be over. All is at rest.

Yes, the great day will arrive when you will casually look at success because you *know* it is there, not because you wonder whether it is. You will know that *you are,* therefore *it must be.*

Even now you are well on your way. Keep going.

SUCCESSFUL TECHNIQUES FOR SUCCESSFUL DAYS

1. Create your desires in imagination. Faithfully claim them as your own.

2. Realize that creative imagination is faith-in-action.

3. Follow up your verbal and imaginative pictures with practical procedures.

4. Practice the fine art of maintaining verbal visions, regardless of your present viewpoints. Always see yourself as you want to see yourself.

5. Do everything possible to get outside your present self. Go up, over, beyond!

6. Accept the fact that if anyone else can be successful, so can you.

7. Rest in the wonderful truth that you will sooner or later make actualities out of visualizations.

8. Start anywhere you like. Simply start.

9. Encourage yourself with the realization that large successes are bound to follow small ones.

10. Keep going and you'll keep growing!

TALK YOUR WAY TO LIFE LEADERSHIP

Chapter 8

REFUSE TO BE JUST ONE OF THE CHORUS who meekly echoes the cry of the soloist!

To be a leader you must sing out. Never mind whether you feel you have a soloist's voice or not. If you can talk at all, you're in . . . and your leadership qualities are out where you will loftily lead life.

I'd like to tell you a story that will make the rest of the chapter clearer and more helpful. It is more than a story, it is your example. This little adventure didn't actually happen to the people involved, but it can—in your own special way—happen to you. In a way it is a true story for it happens every day.

HAIL THE HERO!

One day in New York City massed flags gaily fluttered over Broadway. The street was lined with cheering throngs. Confetti flew down like rain in a valley. Military bands blared out triumphant marches. Sidewalks shook with the shock of stamping soldiers who stepped down the street.

A hero had come home! Down Broadway he rode on his splendid white horse. "Hail, General Jones!" everyone cheered as he nodded left and right like the great leader he was.

But way, way back, hidden in the ranks among the indistinguishable private soldiers was a certain indistinguishable private soldier. His name was Private Jones, but he bore no relation by either blood or personal characteristics with the great General Jones.

DO YOU ALSO ASK YOURSELF THIS QUESTION?

"How come General Jones is a great hero while I am but a great zero?" Private Jones asked the soldier on his left. But the soldier on his left had no answer for him; neither did the soldier on his right.

When the big parade was over Private Jones miserably dragged himself to the barracks where he mulled the baffling question: "How come General Jones is a great hero while I am but a great zero?" But no one, not even the very wise sergeant, knew the answer.

"Why don't you ask the general himself?" asked a joking soldier.

Private Jones thought it over. "Why not?" he asked himself. "Why not?" he happily answered.

So he polished his rifle and briskly marched up to the general's office. "General Jones," he asked as he smartly saluted, "how come General Jones is a great hero while Private Jones is but a great zero?"

Now General Jones was a very democratic kind of a leader. He didn't mind at all if private soldiers marched into his office with personal problems. Which proved what a truly great hero he was.

HERE IS YOUR ANSWER

"Private Jones," he replied, "to change yourself from a zero to a hero you must learn to talk like a hero. The zero who would become a hero must forget that he is a zero and talk like a hero who is no longer a zero. Do you understand?"

After thinking it over, Private Jones finally figured it out. "You mean that if I *act* like a hero I will soon *be* a hero?"

"*Acts* change *facts,*" the general assured him. "Now I want you to march right out of here and get busy. Start acting like a sergeant or a colonel or even . . ." the general's eyes twinkled, "even like the great general hero that *I* am." The general added with a kindly smile, "Great heroes are needed these days." General Jones then commanded, "Forward march! And I don't want to see Private Jones again until he is better known as *General* Jones!"

But, alas, poor timid Private Jones was frightened by the immensity of the whole thing. He quaked in his boots every time he tried to act like a colonel or a general. He feared that if he opened his mouth someone would close it with a machine-gun.

WAILING AND FAILING GO HAND-IN-HAND

"My environment is too much for me," he wailed. "No one around here will give me an opportunity to be a leader." He wailed and wailed and failed and failed.

So dismal days dragged by for timid Private Jones who was no closer to being a great hero than General Jones was close to being a great zero.

Early one morning a bugle blasted over the barracks and the captain shouted, "On your feet! We're off for the big invasion!" So Private Jones stuffed his barracks bag and climbed up the gangplank into the troopship. For several days they steamed toward the dark waters of the South Pacific until at last they stood offshore of two enemy-held islands—one named *Mok* and the other named *Nok.*

"Take *Mok!*" cried General Jones as he waved his sword. So everyone except Private Jones bravely leaped to the shore.

But Private Jones, in his confusion and misery, thought the command was *Nok,* instead of *Mok,* so when he bravely dashed into the jungles of Nok he found himself all alone. Seeing no enemy soldiers he stood upright and remarked, "Well! What do you know! No enemies at all to frighten me. At least here's *one* place where I can be a hero. Guess I'll start giving orders!"

COMMAND YOUR SPEECH AND YOU'LL HEAR YOUR "ENEMIES" SURRENDER

So he planted himself on a hilltop and shouted with sharp authority: "I'm a hero, not a zero! Does everyone hear and obey?"

To his utter amazement an enemy rifleman timidly climbed down from a palm tree. "I hear and obey," said the enemy soldier as he tossed away his rifle.

To his further astonishment an enemy captain sheepishly crawled from the bushes. "You talk just like a true leader," said the captain as he raised his arms overhead, "and who can disobey a true leader?"

To top the fantastic scene a full-fledged enemy general rushed up frantically waving a white flag. "Big hero," he cried, "I'm *convinced!* Please show me where to sign the surrender papers."

A moment later the anxious General Jones raced up the beach, but his anxiety turned to sheer admiration as he saw ten thousand enemy fingers stabbing the sky.

"You're a hero!" cried General Jones as he pinned sixteen medals to the uniform of Private Jones.

"Well, if you say so," modestly replied our hero.

IT'S ALL BECAUSE **YOU SAY** SO!

"No," exclaimed the general, "because *you* say so! I salute you, Private . . . I mean *General* Jones. And I want you to lead the next parade down Broadway!"

"My first general command," said the newly appointed General Jones as he faced his cheering fellow Americans, "is that every zero will henceforth act like a hero." He added with a kindly smile, "Great heroes are needed these days."

WHAT BROADWAY DO YOU CHOOSE?

Not everyone wants to ride a white horse down Broadway, but there is that certain, special place where you want to lead, to excel. Lead your words and they will lead you down the Broadway of your choice.

If you are now an indistinguishable private citizen submerged in the ranks of millions of other private citizens, you can do just one of two things: stay where you are or march to where you aren't. Whatever kind of army you prefer to lead, wherever you wish to be a conqueror, you can become as much of a hero as you say (and *believe*) you can become. Dr. John A. Schindler writes of this kind of heroism: "Your life *can* be an exhilarating and enthusiastic journey through a golden avenue of days, humming a happy tune. Actually, a life of that kind is just as easy, and infinitely better, than the old way of muddling through."[3]

Word magic and mind power are not methods for kidding yourself but for finding yourself. You will like what you find, for the average person vastly underrates his success-capacities in almost all life endeavor.

Try these tactics for militant leadership:

1. Believe that every zero can become a hero.
2. Remember that your acts (verbal and physical) change facts.
3. Get those hidden "enemies" (who may, in most cases, turn out to be friends in disguise) out into the open by standing up for yourself.
4. Give honor and respect to all men, but not one ounce of fear or awe. You'll charm friends and disarm "enemies."
5. Speak with authority in whatever field you now have even the slightest amount of mastery. Make the most of your present capabilities.
6. Have confidence that you are the master of your present environment. Refuse to quail before any circumstance.
7. Remember that you back yourself up with that needed *feeling* of authority when you speak with authority.
8. Start leading!

[3] John A. Schindler, *How to Live 365 Days a Year* (Englewood Cliffs, N.J.: Prentice-Hall, Inc., 1955).

IT IS EASIER THAN YOU THINK!

To change from failure to success is far simpler than you may imagine. A leader is a leader because he simply—*leads.* If you wish to find those undreamed-of leadership qualities in yourself you must simply—*lead.* Lead your words, lead your acts, lead your attitudes. Self-leading is always the requisite to other-leading.

LEAD YOUR WORDS AND THEY WILL LEAD YOU

Think of your positive words as leaders that powerfully and steadily take you wherever you wish to go. We don't ride in stage-coaches anymore, but slip back into history just long enough to picture yourself at the reins of a waiting stage-coach. You shout the command and the word-horses leap forward. As you continue to direct them you successfully pass through dark woods, climb rugged peaks, cross bony deserts. You have no worry, no tension, no fear, for your stage-coach will take the exact turns which you command. After a while you break into the lush, green valley of your destination. You arrive.

You have heard this idea of changing your words and responses many times before in this book . . . and you will hear it again and again . . . and again. There's a reason! You see, if you lead the usual, the time-worn, the humdrum, you can only look behind at the usual, humdrum results. This makes perfect sense, doesn't it? And doesn't it also make a happier world of sense to realize that by speaking the new, the refreshing, the unexpected, you will score new, refreshing, unexpected victories? Of course. You must break away from your *old* self in order to stand afar and see your *new* self.

THERE IS ABSOLUTELY NOTHING TO STOP YOU—EXCEPT YOURSELF

Poor Private Jones had to struggle along in pained bewilderment for a long time because he didn't know what you now know. He didn't know that his trap was self-sprung. He accidentally stumbled upon success, but you can do it the easy way. The easy way is simply to:

DO THE UNUSUAL—AND SCORE A SMASHING VICTORY

If you stop long enough to ask your mental habit-system why you can't do the unusual—and so win out—the only accurate reply it could make is, "Well . . . because . . . *you have just never done it before,* that's why."

WHICH IS THE BEST REASON **FOR** DOING IT!

If the idea of doing great things sounds unusual to you, you are very fortunate, for you know very well that your deep desire *is* to do the unusual. You *do* want to get out of the rut, you *do* want to shoot your life up to that unusually high plane. Could anything be clearer?

WHAT HAPPENED WHEN STONEWALL JACKSON DID THE UNUSUAL

I now want to tell you a soldier story that actually happened.

Early on a May morning in 1863 the great Christian general of the Confederacy, Stonewall Jackson, woke up with a bold plan that was to result in one of the most brilliant Southern victories of the Civil War.

Jackson's keen mind was saturated with but one desire—to smash the opposing army of the Northern commander, General Joseph E. Hooker. But how to do it? Hooker, though certainly not the best of the Union commanders, was certainly no fool. He was expecting something from that pair of gray foxes, Lee and Jackson. So what could Stonewall do? Just one thing—the *unusual.* The usual would bring only expected resistance, but a single, unexpected blow might drive the Union army from

Confederate soil forever. So this was his plan in one word—the *unusual.*

"I propose," Stonewall stated to Robert E. Lee (I am paraphrasing their actual conversation), "to strike the enemy on the right flank. My reports show that an attack on Hooker's right wing could lead to a crumpling of the entire Federal line."

Lee's eyes brightened. "And how will you accomplish this?" he asked (and note that Lee didn't ask *if* he could do it, only *how* he would do it).

Jackson spread out a map and traced his proposed march. It was a fantastically daring maneuver that would place Jackson's men in the perfect position to fall like a sledgehammer on the unsuspecting Union right flank. "With speed and care we may chase them back to Washington," Jackson pointed out.

"And what troops do you propose to use?" asked Lee with mounting anticipation.

"My entire corps," Jackson answered.

Lee considered the unusual strategy. It was amazing boldness for it meant that Jackson's departure would leave Lee with but 14,000 troops with which to face the enemy's overwhelming total of 50,000.

DON'T FEAR TO TRY SOMETHING NEW

But Lee, like Jackson, knew the importance of doing the unusual in order to produce unusual victories. "You may proceed, General," Lee told Jackson. "Meanwhile we'll try to keep those people over there busily preparing for the usual."

Jackson prayed—and marched. Silently, swiftly he led his men in a long swing toward the right wing of the opposing army. As they grimly pushed closer and closer the dozing enemy troops were totally unalarmed for they were concerned only with the usual. They looked up in only mild surprise as frightened deer and rabbits dashed through their camp, chased by the approaching men in gray.

"Eeee-ooo!" the Southern battle-cry shrieked from thousands of throats. The Confederate army hurled itself upon the unguarded right flank. The shocked Northerners leaped to their guns—but too late. Their blue line sagged . . . and broke. The attackers rolled over them with smothering fury . . . and the battle was all but over.

The battle of Chancellorsville was won by brave Southerners, by daring leaders . . . and by the *unusual.*

WHEN **YOU** ARE DIFFERENT—**THINGS** ARE DIFFERENT

No doubt you have often wondered why it is that some folks consistently win life's victories. You know that they, like you, also face daily challenges. But you ask, "How is it they are always on top? What have they got that I haven't got?" There is only one possible answer: *They made circumstances different by making themselves different.*

So change your strategy. Make new plans. Break away from the time-worn. Change yourself and let circumstances change with you. The only difference between a melody and a noise is the musician.

Adopt this attitude: "I will speak, that I may be refreshed." (Job 32:20)

Refresh yourself at this very moment by reading the following aloud:

"To be different, I must speak differently. When I switch my speech from the usual to the unusual I will have unusual results. I will do so at every opportunity."

Now repeat some of the affirmations you have already added to your vocabulary.

HOW TO TALK YOUR WAY TO LIFE LEADERSHIP

I now want to give you a single, all-powerful idea that may well revolutionize your life. It is a truth that is either consciously or subconsciously accepted by every person who has risen above the commonplace. When you understand and apply it you will elevate yourself in a way that will astound you. It is a very special technique for doing the unusual. This idea—let's call it a proven, operative Law of Life—is:

THINK, BELIEVE, AND DECLARE THAT YOUR SUCCESS MAY COME FROM A SOURCE THAT IS NOW UNKNOWN TO YOU

Leave yourself wide open to the unfamiliar, the novel, the daring. Believe that there are much greater things in store for you. (This is an actual fact at the present moment, but you must believe it—and act accordingly—before it can objectify itself to you.)

Never say that your success *must* come from this or that source. Never agree that if this particular endeavor fails you will fail with it. Never tell yourself that you must have *this* friend or *that* man or *this* woman in order to be happy, but rather declare that every closed door means an opportunity to open a larger one. Believe this to be the truth, regardless of what your reasoning tells you, for it is limited reasoning.

The booming business is waiting for the man who accepts a successful self and ignores circumstances.

A new love is just around the corner for the woman who refuses to be crushed by a past heartache.

Undreamed-of riches are already on hand for the courageous man or woman who believes they are there.

Never wonder whether something is too good to be true, but rather wonderfully declare that it *is* true and always good for you.

"What things soever ye desire, when ye pray, believe that ye receive them, and ye shall have them." (Mark 11:24) This is either true or untrue. Which do you prefer to believe?

FORGET CLOSED DOORS—OPEN **YOURSELF**

Never quit. Never give up. Never complain. Never run off, for when you try to escape you bring yourself with you and make your new circumstances exactly as they were before. *You* are always your *circumstances.*

You need never concern yourself with a closed door: all you need is an open faith. When you lead yourself toward your palace with the calm expectation of entering, the doors will magically open before you.

A junior executive, an effective leader in the meat-packing business, once told me, "I have developed a world-winning technique for building those leadership qualities which my position requires. I'd just as soon go without dinner as do without it."

When I pressed him for details he continued, "Once every week I receive a letter chock-full of good news. It includes practical suggestions for the efficient handling of my affairs, plus messages of strength and confidence. It never fails to fire my imagination with greater and greater possibilities. And the possibilities have a strange way of making themselves actualities."

"Sounds great," I commented. "Who writes them?"

He smiled as he tapped his forefinger on his chest. "*I* write them."

UNUSUAL AND EFFECTIVE

"You write a weekly letter to yourself?" I mused. "Sounds unusual."

"And *effective,*" he declared. "You'd be surprised how well it works. You see, whenever I sit down to write I consider the next few days ahead of me. Knowing that I need certain powers for certain lines of action I slant the letter to fit my need. Sometimes it's boldness, sometimes patience, sometimes just plain good humor. As soon as I determine the special type of push I need I pick up my pen and go to work—and when it returns to me through the mail it goes to work on *me.*" He paused and asked, "Like to see one?"

His enthusiasm was enough to convince me but I wanted to see exactly how it was accomplished, so I read his letter, which went something like this:

> Dear Mr. Lawrence:
>
> In a few days you will attend the monthly executives' conference. You will prepare for it to the very best of your abilities—which, incidentally, are considerable.

You will enter into discussions with complete confidence, you will be courteously bold.

When your opinions are requested you will say exactly what you think. From time to time you will also volunteer enlightening comments and suggestions. Since you are there to offer contributions, your contributions will command full respect.

You will carefully consider the opinions and judgments of your associates, but if you can propose a superior plan of action you will speak up without hesitation. Your alternative proposals will be based on intelligent reasonings and up-to-date knowledge.

You will be alert, you will know exactly what you are doing every moment. You know what you want.

At all times you will be relaxed and good-humored. You have handled tough problems before and you will take charge of the present ones in the same serene spirit.

It is a happy fact that you will emerge from the conference with a deep sense of self-satisfaction. You will have an equally high regard for the valuable contributions of your associates.

Remember, Mr. Lawrence: "Be strong and of a good courage; be not afraid, neither be thou dismayed: for the Lord thy God is with thee withersoever thou goest." [Joshua 1:9]

Very truly yours,
B. D. Lawrence

No doubt you know that every time you read certain New Testament books you are reading letters—St. Paul's Epistle to the Romans and others. Here is mail we certainly wouldn't dream of doing without! You need not be a St. Paul to send yourself letters that will enable you to see yourself as God already sees you—as a potential leader in whatever place you may be. So write yourself—with either pen or imagination—and expect to see yourself as a winner. You will not be disappointed, for it is still basic psychology that, "If thou canst believe, all things are possible to him that believeth." (Mark 9:23) And Claude M. Bristol, a writer on modern psychology, excellently states: "Just believe that there is genuine creative magic in believing—and magic there will be, for belief will supply the power which will enable you to succeed in everything you undertake."[4]

READY . . . AIM . . . FIRE!

A psychologist once combined dramatics with humor by entering the lecture platform with a small black bag. Setting it in full view of the audience he remarked, "I am going to show you how to shoot your way through all those nagging obstacles in your life." He smilingly inquired, "Are you ready to fire?"

As the audience curiously watched he opened the bag and pulled out a toy pistol. Shaking his head he set it aside. Next he pulled out some toy bullets and set them aside with another shake of his head.

He finally pulled out a dictionary, held it up, nodded in satisfaction, smiled, remarked, "Here is your stockpile of live ammunition . . . your *words.* We are now ready to shoot our way free from all those enemy prison-camps in our lives."

He then proceeded to speak on the power of everyday language for building free and strong qualities of life leadership.

HOW TO BUILD YOUR STOCKPILE OF LIVE AMMUNITION

With this idea in mind, let me pass on to you an interesting and workable method for keeping your verbal arsenal well filled.

Whenever you find yourself speaking, thinking, or feeling ideas of defeat, immediately shoot back with at least two other words that mean just the opposite. You will be able to reach for them more quickly by using counterattacking words that start with the same letter as the problem word, for example:

Tension is released with **tenderness** and **trust.**
Negativity is banished with **newness** and **nobility.**
Depression is conquered with **daring** and **determination.**

[4] Claude M. Bristol, *The Magic of Believing* (Englewood Cliffs, N. J.: Prentice-Hall, Inc., 1957).

Bitterness is beaten with **brightness** and **blessing.**
Complaint is conquered with **courage** and **cheeriness.**

Become a sharpshooter! Whenever you feel yourself under attack by nerves or worry or frustration, start your counter-attack with heroic words and phrases. It is impossible for you to run out of ammunition, so freely fire away, use as much as you can as often as you can. You will soon have all those "enemies" on the run!

And you will be a leader.

IMPRESS YOURSELF WITH THESE LIFE-LEADERSHIP TRUTHS

1. Talk and act like the leader you want to be!

2. Assert that you now have heroic qualities which will lead you to triumph over all circumstances.

3. Bear in mind that positive verbal, mental, and physical acts change negative facts.

4. Think of your words as powerful leaders which surely draw you to your desired destinations.

5. To see unusual results . . . dare to do the unusual.

6. Resolve to be different from what you are.

7. Know that a new you will automatically create new circumstances.

8. Look for expected victories in unexpected places! Expand your victory visions.

9. Ignore closed doors. Open yourself.

10. Be a verbal sharpshooter . . . and you will hit your targets!

HAPPY EMOTIONS THROUGH HAPPY SPEECH!

Chapter 9

A DESPERATELY UNHAPPY WOMAN told her minister, "My problem is easy to state but difficult to understand. Here it is: How do I switch from unhappiness to happiness?"

"To move from the one to the other," he replied, "you must change your subconscious beliefs about yourself and your relation to life from the unhappy to the happy, that is, from the negative to the positive. You must have an emotional state which is based on reality and mature attitudes. You must be honestly pleased with yourself in spite of your shortcomings. We might sum up by saying that *you must learn to recognize happiness when you see it.*"

Let's break into this conversation long enough to add some authoritative weight to these conclusions. Dr. Hornell Hart reveals: "It has been found that whether a person is joyful or miserable depends not merely or even mostly on what happens to him, but rather on the attitudes he takes."[1]

Dr. Hart tells of hundreds of folks who found that their unhappiness was—in a large measure—merely an illusion created by false outlooks. But when their subconscious minds were trained to recognize happiness as a reality, happiness *was* a reality. Gladness steadily replaced gloom.

[1] Hornell Hart, *Autoconditioning* (Englewood Cliffs, N.J.: Prentice-Hall, Inc., 1956).

SO THIS IS YOUR GOAL—MENTAL AND EMOTIONAL STATES THAT RECOGNIZE HAPPINESS AS A REALITY

"This is great news for you," the minister continued, "for it means that once you attain these joy-recognizing states you will automatically live happily, regardless of surrounding circumstances. This may sound absurdly simple; perhaps that is why so many folks miss it."

"So the whole idea is to change my emotions," she made the inevitable deduction. "But how do I do it? My feelings always seem to have the best of me."

PICTURE YOUR EMOTIONS AS RIVERS

"First of all," he told her, "picture all your emotions as rivers which seek outlets on the broad sea of your life. Some of these rivers enter your life as peaceful currents which will gently move you toward your desired harbors; others are raging torrents which toss you about and upset you."

"I get the picture," she assented.

PICTURE YOUR WORDS AS THE HELM

"Secondly," he continued, "think of your daily words as the helm of your ship-of-life. Every time you speak correctly you turn your ship into serene currents. Is that clear?"

She smiled. "And *inviting*."

"Good. The next time you walk down the street I want you to pretend that you are sailing through life. Imagine that you meet several folks who ask you how you are doing. You will immediately tell them that you are sailing along very nicely, the ship is under perfect control, your voyage is even now a pleasant one. Now open yourself to feelings that correspond with your declarations."

This idea produced another smile. "You know what? . . . I do this all the time. I mean, I frequently hold imaginary conversations. I notice that almost everyone does."

THIS OLD HABIT CAN BE USED TO BUILD NEW AND PLEASURABLE HABITS

"It's a ready-made device," he told her. "That's why it's so effective. Just make sure you respond in a positive manner. It's as easy as that. Come back and see me after sailing your steady course for a while."

A month later he asked her, "How do you feel?"

"Just fine!" she jubilantly exclaimed. "I really do!"

"Are you still meeting invisible friends?"

"Strangely enough, no," she replied. "It's no longer necessary."

"How come?"

She happily waved her hands. "Because I do it with *real* people. It's amazing but as I began to talk the way I wanted to feel I began to feel the way I talked."

"How come?" the minister repeated.

"Because happy talk makes happy emotions!"

"You mean it's the *real thing?* You really *are* happy?"

"Yes, and for heaven's sake I was happy all along but just didn't know it. At first I thought I was kidding myself into a false state of happiness but I discovered that I was really kidding myself when I spoke words of defeat and futility."

What happened to her? She had simply discovered a truth that someone once expressed in this way: "Most people are much happier than they think they are."

TAKE **THIS** ATTITUDE AND YOU WILL SEE **ALL** YOUR ATTITUDES CHANGE TO SATISFACTION AND HAPPINESS

Take the attitude that all attitudes—all feelings—of unhappiness are *false* and that all attitudes of happiness are *true* and you will be amazed at the steady improvement of your happiness-level. You will learn something you may never have known before—that you are truly the master of your own feelings, that you can be happy by commanding happiness. It is not so much that you create happiness but that you reveal something that was secretly there all along.

YOUR JOY CAN BE A CERTAINTY!

Happiness is the acceptance of happy emotions in place of unhappy ones. If you can absorb the one you can also absorb the other. It is of utmost importance that you believe this or you will not get off the ground.

Everyone is fully capable of accepting much more of pleasure-pulsating emotions. Your happiness-level will rise in equal proportion to your acceptance of the truth that joy can be your certainty.

Think of happiness as a personal faculty which you can exercise at will.

Think of your words as the right exercises.

"I WILL . . . POUR YOU OUT A BLESSING"

"If I could deliver but one lecture in my life," declared a prominent counsellor, "I would pound home the single truth that anyone can have as much happiness in life as he will accept from life. It is never a question of struggling, only of accepting. It is never a question of shaking your fist at the world but one of opening your palm. How very few really believe or practice this."

It is sad but true that the great majority of folks are unhappy because of a secret and subconscious "clinched-fist" policy which can only result in increased bitterness, tension, and frustration. But when you switch to the "open-palm" policy you then receive the promise, "I will . . . open you the windows of heaven, and pour you out a blessing, that there shall not be room enough to receive it." (Malachi 3:10)

To a friend I suggested the daily habit of deliberately opening his hand to form a receptive palm, while affirming the eagerness of life to fill it with good things. He said it worked out in a practical way; it gave him new powers of enthusiasm and courage which he was then able to return as powers on the job and in friendships.

Apply this "open-palm" policy and you will penetrate the age-old (but rarely understood) principle that happiness does not depend upon circumstances but rather on your feelings and attitudes toward them. You will also triumphantly answer the question as to why one person can be truly happy in the very same circumstance that dejects another.

HAPPINESS IS THE WAY **YOU** ARE, NOT THE WAY **THINGS** ARE

It is the way you are, not the way things are. You have proved this ten thousand times. If you do not feel content without a bright new automobile you will never be happy simply by getting one. You will get a bright new car and nothing more.

The physical cannot replace the spiritual. Happiness—a spiritual quality—must be satisfied by spiritual means and an automobile is purely mechanical. Your new automobile can give you a smooth ride only if you are riding smoothly before you get into it.

AN OPEN PALM IS MEANT TO BE FILLED . . . SO OPEN YOURSELF RIGHT NOW

Whenever feelings of hopelessness or despair seek lodging in your inner being, picture yourself as calmly standing with open palm, ready and eager to receive the happiness that is now coming your way. Your happy feelings will follow your pictured action. Try the following word-play:

Think of life-giving words that start with the same letters as are in your name. For example, if your name is Richard, you might supply *resolute* and *resourceful* for the letter *R*. For the letter *i* you could come up with *ideal* and *ingenious*. This personal application will provide you with personal qualities, for as you gain a new *consciousness* of the ideal you *become* that of which you are conscious.

HERE IS MORE GOOD NEWS: HAPPY ATTITUDES MAGICALLY CHANGE OUTER CIRCUMSTANCES

Believe this proven principle:

> **By creating positive feelings within yourself while in your present circumstances, you can actually change those circumstances into what you want. You magically draw to yourself those elements you need for a more prosperous life.**

AFFIRM THIS

Repeat this affirmation until it turns into an emotional force: "When *I* am right, *things* are right. By encouraging good feelings I start a chain of events which create good circumstances. I daily practice this principle because I firmly believe in it. When *I* am right, *things* are right."

It is basic psychology that an emotionalized situation has the tendency to become an objective reality. The football team that feels victorious is on the way to achieving victory on the field. The man or woman who first has an inner alliance with happiness magically steps forth to receive additional blessing in outer circumstances. Psychologist William James repeatedly affirmed the powers of constructive emotions to build the constructive life.

Since happiness is the way we feel, and the way we feel is largely determined by the way we talk, it is perfectly logical that you can talk yourself into soaring levels of well-being.

A man told me he thought of happiness-building through word power as a game of tag. "I tag myself with sunny words all day long . . . and run like a rabbit whenever someone tries to tag me with gloom. I win the game every time!"

DO LIKEWISE!

Tag yourself with every sunny word possible! Refuse to be caught by depressing remarks from yourself or from others.

Don't join in dreary discussions, reject gloom and negativity whenever and wherever it tries to tag you.

IF YOU SAY THAT WE MUST FACE REALITY IN A REALISTIC WORLD . . .

Some may ask, "But isn't this simply an escape from reality? Must we not face life as it is?"

It depends upon what you believe life is. You will not be avoiding reality when you do this; in truth you will be avoiding unreality—for the overwhelming number of gloomy prophecies never happen. And when some of them do occur you may be sure that they were induced by the very intensity of attention to them.

Your goal is to create *new, enriching* realities.

WEAR HAPPINESS AS A HABIT

A lecturer in Dallas had just concluded a talk entitled, "Wear Happiness as a Habit" when a man from the audience approached him on the stage.

"I don't know about that lecture of yours," the man said as he doubtfully shook his head. "It seems that you're asking the impossible. How can I wear happiness as a habit when it doesn't seem to fit my nature?"

The lecturer touched the man's suit. "This suit you're wearing . . . did you know it fitted you before you tried it on?"

"No, of course not."

"Does it fit you now?"

"Yes. Perfectly."

"How do you know?"

The man vaguely gestured. "Why . . . because I *wear* it."

"So you now feel it to be a satisfactory, well-fitting suit?"

"Right."

"And it *always* fits you, doesn't it? . . . no matter what the weather?"

"Yes," the man agreed, "it's a fine suit for both sunny and stormy days."

HAPPINESS **DOES** SUIT YOU

"All right," the lecturer pressed his point, "how about your suitability for happiness? Do you think you can have happiness as an everyday experience before you try it on?"

"I don't know," the inquirer confessed, "I'm emotionally mixed up."

"The only reason a peaceful life doesn't suit you is because you keep taking it off every time a stormy sky appears. I suggest you try wearing happiness as a habit in all kinds of weather, just as you wear that suit of yours."

"Show me how," the man challenged.

The lecturer nodded. "Stop telling yourself that you are at the mercy of the changing weather, for every time you do so you actually expose yourself. Do you know what happens every time you declare yourself a helpless victim of the weather of life?"

"What?"

"You unbutton your well-fitting suit of happiness. You expose yourself to every imaginable storm. You get drenched by the very feelings you want to keep out. You further convince yourself that happiness just doesn't suit you. Which is all wrong."

A new understanding broke over the man's face. "How could I have missed such a fundamental fact as that?"

The lecturer continued. "Let me show you how to bring your desired emotions in line. From now on I want you to think of every spoken word as a button."

The man smiled in amusement. "A *button?* I think I get it."

BUTTON UP!

"Every time you run into a threatening storm immediately button up your suit of happiness with words that proclaim complete protection. Declare that you are untouchable. Try something like, 'My happiness is suitable in *all* weather,' or 'Here's an opportunity to prove the value of my protective clothing.' You may be sure that happiness will become a habit."

"Put on the suit and keep it well buttoned," the man gratefully chuckled.

"It will suit you so well you will never again take it off."

REVIEW THESE FOUR FACTS

Before you receive other helpful ideas for inducing happy emotions I would like you to review these four pertinent facts:

1. When you have an emotionally unhappy attitude toward a person or circumstance or yourself . . .

2. You reinforce your unhappiness every time you speak unhappily about it, however . . .

3. You can change the depressing feeling and charge yourself with positive power by . . .

4. Speaking and thinking in an opposite manner—with cheery words and thoughts.

WORDS ARE BREEDERS—BREED ONLY WHAT IS GOOD FOR YOU

You waste precious moments of your life every time you utter wasteful words, so determine that you will be self-determining, that you will breed only the lovely, only the strong. One wrong word can not only ruin your entire day but will falsely convince you that following days must be borne with the same misery.

Unhappiness–like happiness–always breeds itself. It's like the miserable man who sent his photo to a lonely hearts' club, only to have it returned with the sad note, "We're not *that* lonely!"

SNIP AWAY THOSE CHAINED FEELINGS!

Imagine your words as being sharp snippers. Imagine that every time you speak a positive phrase you snip off a link of those life-binding chains.

"It will be done!" *Snip!*
"I am unlimited!" *Snip!*
"Victory is mine!" *Snip!*

"I enjoy happiness, peace, faith, courage, relaxation!" *Snip! Snip! Snip! Snip! Snip!*

This is a proven technique that has produced remarkable results in many lives. I want you to practice it for yourself so that you will personally know what you are talking about.

FREE YOUR EMOTIONS THROUGH FREE SPEECH

Inhibited speech is the enemy of your state of liberty. No doubt you can recall dozens of times when you wanted to express your honest, heart-felt feelings about something but you held back for fear of what others would think or even what you would think of yourself. It gave you a vague, uncomfortable feeling; even made you dislike yourself for your timidity. Most of them were little things, but they disturbed in a big way.

The boy wants to tell the girl that he is fond of her . . . but fears it may bring ridicule or rejection.

The employee desperately desires a transfer to another job . . . but wonders whether it will impair his future with the company.

The tired bookkeeper wants to relax in front of his TV set . . . but thinks it may be impolite to tell his guests so.

YOU'LL BE SURPRISED HOW WELL THINGS WORK OUT WHEN YOU HONESTLY STATE YOUR CASE

The boy should tell the girl. She is possibly dying to echo his words!

The employee should talk over that transfer. The company may have just the spot for him!

The bookkeeper should politely tell his guests that he doesn't want to miss his favorite program. They might enjoy it too!

WHEN YOU FRANKLY EXPRESS YOUR NEED YOU HAVE TAKEN THE FIRST GOOD STEP TOWARD FULFILLING THAT NEED

Here is an everyday example of this need for expressing your needs. A woman once phoned a well-known author to request that he review a book she had written. When he assured her he could spare the time she gave a huge, audible sigh of relief. When he asked her about the sigh she laughed, "You know, it took me six months to get up enough courage to state my need. I now wish I had done so six months ago!"

You have certain needs in life. Some, like love, approval, self-esteem, friendship, are on a permanent basis. You cannot be fully satisfied unless they are satisfied. Others, like recreation, humor, and solitude are required from time to time.

But whatever you need, you will never fully acquire it until you frankly state your need for it.

(This is a tricky idea, for the human mind is highly skilled in the art of self-deception. A tensely driving businessman might scornfully remark, "Who needs approval from the world? All I want is its money." He fails to realize that he wants wealth for the very purpose of attracting attention and approval.)

DECLARE YOUR FREEDOM OF SPEECH!

All your life you have been wondering what others think . . . and it usually makes you miserable. It imprisons and frustrates you. You will never be emotionally free until you talk a free language, until you load it with honest, freely flowing expression. This is the sure-fire way of building your self-respect, for revealing yourself as the independent thinker you want to be.

Never fear rejection of your honest expressions, for no one can reject you unless you accept their rejection. Uninhibited speech is a means for accepting yourself and projecting yourself as you want to see yourself and as you want others to see you.

HOW YOUR WORD POWER WILL RELEASE YOU FROM EMOTIONAL FRUSTRATION

"I come to you as a last resort," a department-store manager told his doctor. "I am a bundle of nerves and frustrations simply because I am afraid of letting myself go, of speaking my mind. I'm an emotional poker-face. I have analyzed my problem enough to know that I need more honest self-expression. In short, I want to laugh more, show affection, sympathize, shout, even get a little rowdy at times. Can you take it from there? Can you show me how to break through?"

"Relax," his doctor told him, "your problem is as commonplace as it is troublesome. Half the folks who come in here are frozen with the same emotional ice as you, though they are not as aware of it."

"Then something can be done?"

TALK YOUR WAY TO CONSTANT FEELINGS OF DELIGHT

"*Everything* can be done. Your shut-mouth policy got you into this jam but an open-mouth policy will release you. Tell me," asked the doctor, "do you usually speak first when you meet a casual acquaintance?"

"No, I usually wait to see if he also recognizes me."

"After this, be the first to speak up. Never mind whether he recognizes you. Do you ever tell folks that you need and appreciate them?"

"Rarely. I'd rather wait until I'm sure that *I'm* appreciated."

"Step boldly up and tell them. You're in for some delightful experiences. Do you ever tell jokes at a party?"

"I don't know any."

"I'll give you some of my stale ones. They won't make you a first-class comedian but they'll take you out of your third-class social position. Tell me, where do you usually sit in church?"

"Near the back. I guess I'm self-conscious."

"Sit in a front row. Let others enjoy your very fine appearance. But I suggest you carry a damp handkerchief in case the pastor faints at seeing you so close."

The man grinned in a combination of delight and amazement. "You must be a mind-reader. All those things are exactly what I *want* to do. I *do* want to be the friendly type, I *do* want others to enjoy me. Do you mean to tell me that these ten-cent timidities are the things that gang up on me?"

"Exactly. Let me illustrate it for you. Would you give me a dime if I asked for one?"

"Yes."

"Would you give me five dimes?"

"Probably."

"Would you give me fifty dimes?"

"No."

"Why not?"

He grinned. "It's too much. I can't afford it."

YOU CANNOT AFFORD TO REPRESS HONEST EMOTION

"Neither can you afford all of those ten-cent timidities. If you will speak up on these ten-cent occasions you will gradually earn yourself a million dollars worth of emotional relaxation. To be emotionally free you must speak in an emotionally free manner. Think of the honest expression of your inner desires as Relief Responses, for that is exactly what they are. Every time you loosen yourself ever so little from your stilted speech habits you will feel a corresponding measure of emotional release."

The man carried out the counsel and reported, "What a relief! Not only do I respect myself much more but I see a new respect for me in the eyes of others. Verbal courage is a wonder-worker!"

LEARN THE DIFFERENCE BETWEEN "HUMAN DIGNITY" AND HUMAN FREEDOM

Every time you fail to release your inner desires you build up within yourself a tiny packet of resentment. You feel cheated. Understand that repression is not dignity, it is self-deception. It was difficult for the above-mentioned man to face this truth for he preferred to think of himself as a dignified, conservative individual who was above such things as attracting attention with a party joke. He could kid his conscious mind but he couldn't kid his emotions. His misery found him out.

The world needs less false human dignity and more true

human beings. The good angels are those who are not afraid to come down to earth.

HONEST SPEECH IS POSITIVE SPEECH!

Do you see how free self-expression neatly falls in line with the idea of positive speaking? Unexpressed desires produce negativity, but a forthright externalization of your true feelings will free your positive powers for positive living.

BUT NEVER EXPRESS FEELINGS OF HOPELESSNESS, FOR THEY ARE DISHONEST FEELINGS

Of course you have daily challenges that cause you to feel chained. Believe that they are dishonest evaluations! Regardless of how seemingly permanent are the chains of worry and despair, convince yourself that you can break free by faithfully applying your word-power techniques.

Speaking hopelessly is like putting pepper on ice cream; anyone can do it but who wants it?

TRY THIS TEN-CENT TECHNIQUE FOR A MILLION DOLLARS WORTH OF LIFE-LIBERTY

Clip a dozen or more tiny slips of paper and write your new verbal braveries on them. They can be anything that will enable you to take those first steps toward emotional liberty. Perhaps you can remind yourself to make a bold business call, maybe you wish to tell someone how important he is to you—anything, just as long as it is something that you really wish you *could* say. Be absolutely honest, absolutely fearless.

Place your slips in a jar. Now speak your desires a little at a time. Take it easy. Relax about the whole thing. But speak up. Say what you want to say. Timidly, perhaps, at first, but express yourself as you wish to express yourself. Forget what others will think, remember only what you want to say.

Every time you speak up—and *regardless of the result of your verbal courage*—remove the slip from the jar and replace it with a dime.

By the time you have about five dollars in the jar you may also have a million dollars worth of new heroism and self-command.

As a final step, take your five dollars and buy yourself a small present—something you've always wanted to buy!

BOUNTIFUL BLESSING THROUGH BOUNTIFUL SPEECH

David Livingstone, that great missionary-explorer, once trudged into the deep African hills to find a remote tribe carrying buckets of water from the river to their fields.

"Why don't you simply release the full blessings of the river so that it might bountifully serve you?" he asked as he stood on the river bank.

"But how can we?" they asked, "when the river is here and our fields are over there?"

Livingstone took a stick and quickly cut the ground so that a trickle of water rushed from the river toward the fields. "Like this!" he exclaimed.

The natives were amazed at the simple logic of a channel. Like delighted schoolboys they connected the river with their fields.

Perhaps you have never thought of your words as channels of self-blessing. Think of them as deep channels that release a full, free flow of emotional power.

Your harvest will be bountiful.

HIGHLIGHTS FOR HIGH SPIRITS

1. Use word power to sail through life on peaceful emotions.

2. Emphatically assert that happiness can be a certainty in every department of your life. Deny all appearances to the contrary.

3. Realize that a present concept of a happy self will magically turn circumstances into delightful ones.

4. Don't struggle. Adopt the open-palm policy.

5. Affirm, believe, "When I am right, things are right."

6. For sunny days, tag yourself with sunny words!

7. Know that happiness does suit your nature.

8. Use positive word power to snip away those false feelings of frustration. Talk yourself out of it!

9. Don't stunt your emotional growth by refusing to admit your basic needs.

10. Enrich yourself with a million dollars worth of life and liberty by speaking up on ten-cent occasions.

TALK YOURSELF INTO NEW ENERGY AND CREATIVE POWER

Chapter 10

A MAN WAS ONCE ASKED, "CAN YOU play the piano?"

"I don't know," he replied, "I've never tried."

Perhaps you have never tried to do many of the things you desire to do because you have never thought of trying . . . or because you are just plain tired.

Without enthusiasm, bounce, and high hopes you will stumble along the same old way, perhaps never quite giving up but never quite making it either. But with a full measure of strength that springs from a zealous heart you can do great things which you never thought possible. "Give me a man with a fired-up spirit," says a corporation executive, "and I will show him how to light up his world."

I want to give you several sharp ideas for firing up powers that you now posesses so that you may also burn brightly in whatever world you choose.

HOW BESSIE SWITCHED FROM THE BORING TO THE SOARING

"I'm exhausted from doing nothing," confessed Bessie B., a homemaker. "Practically everything I do is a dull, uninteresting task. Even picnics and parties leave me with a depressed, dissatisfied feeling. No matter where I look I see emptiness. I can hardly wait for bedtime so I can sink into the oblivion of sleep."

"In other words, Bessie," remarked her counsellor, "you are just plain bored."

"Bored stiff. And there's nothing like monotony to knock you out. I realize this is a senseless way to live because I know lots of folks who flit through their days with genuine energy and enthusiasm. But what can I do with my own restlessness?"

THERE IS ABSOLUTELY NO REASON FOR MONOTONY

"There is no good reason why you should dwell in boredom. You have just admitted this by mentioning folks who are truly alive to life. These busy people are living proofs that life can be as grand as you make it. Understand, Bessie, that life itself is not dull, it is just that confused folks have a dull viewpoint. And do you know how they *keep* themselves in boredom?"

"How?"

"By *talking* bored. There is no better way to *feel* lifeless than to talk about it. Just chatter about every idle, despairing thing in your life and you will bore your way right into the center of hopelessness."

"But," she objected, "I'm *naturally* inclined toward negativity."

NO ONE IS **NATURALLY** NEGATIVE

"No," he also objected, "you are never naturally inclined toward anything of a depressing nature. You simply slipped into the habit without knowing it. I can show you how to retrain yourself so that you will have all the benefits of hopeful speech. Tell me, Bessie, do you listen to your radio as you go about your home affairs?"

"Every day."

"Do you switch stations now and then?"

"Several times."

"Why?"

"Oh, I guess because I don't like what I'm hearing. News of international squabbles makes me nervous, dreary music depresses me."

"So you switch them off? You listen to another program?"

"Yes."

"And then you feel better?"

"Yes. Much better."

BROADCAST HAPPY PROGRAMS!

"Good. During the next few weeks I want you to think of your speech as types of radio programs. Whenever you hear something you don't like, switch it off, turn to a cheery program. Create programs that are full of life, zest, beauty. Talk to yourself and to others about Jimmy's good school grades, express your enjoyment of that crisp salad you had for lunch, take verbal pleasure in everything pleasurable. If you keep tuned to these lively programs you will catch an aroma of a sweetly scented life. And you won't be bored or tired or depressed any longer."

Bored Bessie found that positive words are clever magicians —they make a dismal life disappear. She became Bouncy Bessie.

If you also feel constantly tired and restless, know that tired and restless speech is doing it to you. So switch your heart, mind, and tongue to all those wonderful programs that fill the air about you. Repeat them, play them back, play them over, and you will have soaring instead of boring days.

HOW TO BECOME STURDY, TIRELESS, UNSHAKEABLE

A man who courageously confessed that his constant exhaustion was due to faulty speech and thought habits asked me if I could give him a simple plan for reinvigoration.

"When was the last time you walked in the woods?" I asked.

"Three or four months ago on a camping trip."

"What was the dominant feature of those woods?"

"The trees. Thousands of them."

"And you walked among them, enjoyed them?"
"Yes. I'm a nature lover."
"Tell me some of the characteristics of trees."
"Well . . . they're beautiful, grand, graceful."
"Also sturdy, tireless, unshakeable?"
"Yes, trees are strong."

CORRECTLY DESCRIBE YOUR GRAND WORLD!

"When you leave here," I told him, "I want you to constantly think of yourself as walking through a world that consists of a forest of your personal ownership. Look around, give in to feelings of surrounding grandeur. See your world with the same descriptions you gave of trees. Flatly refuse to ever again falsely describe this truly lovely world."

As he nodded I continued. "Now when you go hiking you sometimes come to hills that shut off your view of the trees beyond. Think of these hills as all the tomorrows that you cannot foresee. But continue to joyously walk in the common-sense expectation that not only are there more trees ahead but they are taller, grander, sturdier than the previous ones which belong to you. Know that the farther you walk the better it gets. You will never weary of walking in your forest of towering strength."

ABSORB THE ABUNDANCE OF JOY THAT **NOW** SURROUNDS YOU

If you will also put your mental and verbal emphasis on walking through life with a vigilant sense of surrounding beauty and strength, you will own beauty and strength for yourself.

Don't let a lack of full understanding of this excellent process keep you from practicing it. The happy hiker needs only to start walking in order to find and enjoy the full forest.

Once you know a forest is beautiful, no one and no thing can ever persuade you differently. It is beautiful and you know it . . . you *know.* With new strength you quicken your pace toward the lovelier woods beyond.

POWER AND RESOURCEFULNESS ARE YOURS WHEN YOU BELIEVE THAT YOUR PRESENT POSITION IS A GOOD ONE

Use your verbal vitalities to convince yourself that right now, today, you are in command. *You must believe that your present position is a powerful one, for you always live in the present. There is no other place to live.*

Oh, yes, you want tomorrow to be better. But the way to make tomorrow better is to make today a good day . . . or rather, to make yourself what you should be today. Tomorrow will then become a duplicate of your good today.

How can you use your verbal vitalities to do this? Don't speak words of retreat, don't attack, don't constantly apologize for yourself, stop explaining everything you do, express no worry about opinions and rumors, don't criticize yourself or others, banish suspicious speech . . . and you will have a sturdy framework for building an absolute confidence in your present dwelling.

You like this idea of freeing yourself from the strain of the day, don't you? You like it because it is a way of life that deep down in your heart you wish you could realize. So do it and be done with it! "As thy days, so shall thy strength be." (Deuteronomy 33:25)

"I'M WORN OUT BY TRYING"

A college student once found himself in scholastic trouble. His low grades reached the point where he was in danger of having to leave the campus. In one final attempt at helping himself he set his difficulty before his favorite professor.

"I'm licked," he miserably stated. "No matter how hard I try to run I always fall flat on my face. I'm worn out by trying. Could it really be that I'm not as intelligent as my classmates? I wonder? . . ."

The professor replied, "I understand that you are a topnotch sprinter on the track team. Now it takes a good deal of intelligence to become a star athlete. You certainly must think your way to victory as well as run to it."

The thought brightened the student. "It's good to hear it put that way."

"Your studies are really very similar. Your mental attitude toward racing to high grades in the classroom is just as important as your thoughts when you perform out on the athletic field. But it is evident that you are thinking defeat, for when you came in here you talked of defeat."

"I know," he replied, "but it was an *honest* expression wasn't it? Shouldn't I express what I honestly feel? Isn't that supposed to make me mentally healthy or something?"

"No, not in this case because you were expressing feelings that are entirely unsupported by facts. We have just proved that you are a capable thinker, therefore you have no right to describe yourself as inadequate."

The student wrinkled his forehead. "I'd like to believe that. If I could only find some way to convince myself that I am as tirelessly capable in the classroom as I am on the athletic field."

SEE YOURSELF AS AN ALL-AROUND ATHLETE

"Bring that athletic frame of mind of yours right into the classroom," the professor advised. "Mentally and verbally see yourself as an all-around athlete who leaps all barriers, who jumps fantastic distances, who lightly dashes over the finish line a winner. Make a full and constant use of your verbal vitalities."

His changed speech habits eventually produced a change in his study habits. He raised his grades to the point where he was a scholastic winner as well as a champion on the athletic field.

Try these "all-around athlete" verbal exercises for yourself. If you persist to the end you will no longer find yourself wearied by low grades or long trials or short finances.

SPEAKING OF MONEY . . .

Speaking of money, I have an idea that worry and concern

over the lack of it may be a principal contribution to your general state of irksome weariness.

I now want to make a deposit to your account in the form of a single sentence:

YOU CAN HAVE AS MUCH MONEY AS YOU NEED

Wait! Hold on a minute! It is possible you disagree with this statement. And I agree with you. If you have only a money-lack consciousness it is absolutely impossible for you to agree. Obviously, you can only believe what you believe. And you believe that you tried to get more money and failed, you believe that you can't get more money unless you first get that promotion, you believe that you must save a dollar a day for fifty days in order to have fifty dollars, you believe that an unexpected bill will ruin your budget.

If that's what you *believe,* that's only what you *know* . . . and it is impossible for you to agree with anything else.

Then how do you become wealthy?

By *knowing* different.

And how do you *know* different?

By *being* different.

And how can you *be* different?

By stoutly refusing to believe in yourself as your present limited self and replacing it with a courageously new picture of an enriched self.

This book is purposely loaded with workable word-power techniques that will enable you to do this very thing.

A lack of money is never your parent problem. Inadequate finances are always the children of inadequate attitudes toward money. You should realize with Emerson that, "Money . . . is, in its effects and laws, as beautiful as roses."

INVEST IN RIGHT MENTAL AND VERBAL ATTITUDES AND YOU WILL REAP A RICH PROFIT

It's a funny thing. When we pray for money we usually do it hesitantly, faithlessly, almost as if it is out of God's jurisdiction, yet we boldly pray for the day when the boss will give us a raise. We bewilderedly stand in the wilderness of lack and ask an equally bewildered passerby for the way to Wealth. But the Divine road signs are emphatically clear.

Because we are aware only of the company's abilities to increase our paycheck we hopefully look toward the earthly boss.

But an awareness that God has an unlimited treasury at your command will give you free access to its riches.

"God . . . giveth thee power to get wealth." (Deuteronomy 8:18)

Your earthly boss may or may not be the instrument through which it arrives.

Does it sound interesting enough to look into?

"MAKE YOUR WEALTHY SELF VISIBLE!"

A toy-and-novelty salesman and his wife who were tired of their limited financial condition determined to change their basic attitudes toward money by using word power in this interesting manner: Every time one caught the other expressing money-limiting words—such as complaining about bills or harping about high prices—he immediately said, "I can't see you. Make your wealthy self visible!" The other then quickly replaced words of lack with words of plenty. The other then nodded and said something like, "Oh, there you are—that wealthy person I am getting to know better and better every day."

Their new and optimistic attitudes soon turned into action when they opened a basement workshop in which to create their own original ideas for children's novelties. One of them, a card on which was imprinted several cut-out toys, was instantly accepted for distribution by a leading manufacturer. It sold so well that they were asked for additional ideas which were also successful. As their royalties mounted they invested in first and second trust deeds which further swelled their monthly income. *By daring to believe in a wealthy self they found the ways and means for becoming that in which they believed.*

IF YOU HAVE BEEN STRUGGLING UNSUCCESSFULLY . . .

It is of extreme importance to understand this business of struggle, for mental, emotional, and physical distress always sets in after a violent attempt to do anything.

You will find it easy to maintain constant bounce in your life if you will impress yourself with this idea:

> **The moment you start struggling against anything is the same moment you declare that there is a battle, and the moment you believe there is a battle is the same moment you subconsciously declare that you will lose, for you have been losing in the past and you force yourself to believe that this outcome will also be a defeat. Your belief in failure creates failure. And constant failure wears you down and out.**

Do you remember the story of Joseph in Egypt? Betrayed by his brothers, sold into foreign slavery, cast into the dungeons—here was a man who seemed to have every good reason for losing himself in hate and bitterness. But here was a *man!* He knew—as you should know—that God was on his side. He chose faith instead of fight, humility rather than hate, boldness in place of bitterness. Because he refused to struggle against "cruel fate" he turned his circumstances into such a victory that he became governor of the very land of his imprisonment. Had he chosen to give up he would have gone down in the misery of his unbelief.

GIVE **IN** . . . NOT **UP**

The new order is clear. We must stop struggling against life and start giving in to the Spiritual Laws of Life, for, "The law of the wise is a fountain of life." (Proverbs 13:14)

A psychologist once remarked, "The only difference between success and failure in any sphere of life is the difference between giving in and giving up."

Now what do you suppose he meant? On the surface there doesn't seem to be much difference between the two words, but let's look into it.

You know what *giving up* means. It means abandoning all hope, resignation to "cruel fate," acceptance of second-best. The use of pride is possibly the most common way in which folks give up.

But *giving in* . . . ah! . . . that's another story. You give in when you join a happy conversation with friends, when you learn to do something, when you use a disappointment as an upward step.

Everything good you have ever had in your life came as a result of your giving in . . . when you chose it, when you accepted it, when you took it. Giving in always means a measure of success, a way of getting out of life that which you desire. Giving in always puts good things inside you.

A practical example of this idea of accepting present goodness is that of a New York girl whose vocal career was threatened with collapse because of her refusal to accept advice from her agent concerning her singing style. Her "know-it-all" attitude made it impossible for anyone to help her. One afternoon, while waiting in her agent's office, she had the thrill of meeting an established female vocalist. Their small talk eventually turned to a discussion of the girl's problem. She heard the successful artist confess that she too had once wasted time and opportunities by indulging in petty pride.

"You have your choice of failure-in-pride or success-in-cooperation," was the artist's declaration that jolted the girl into realizing what she was doing to herself. She began to see that her pride was blocking the growth of her natural talents. She knew that the artist's advice was soundly based, for hadn't success come to this woman when she gave in to wise counsel? With this new understanding the girl opened herself to helpful suggestions from all quarters. Her new cooperativeness proved to be a power in itself for giving her career a sharp upward spurt.

GIVE IN, SAY YES TO NEW STRENGTH, AND YOU WON'T MISS OUT ANY LONGER!

Now perhaps you have been missing out too long because you have made a wrong use of the mighty force of your words. You have been speaking a language that causes you to give up instead of in. But it is not at all an exaggeration to state that a simple replacement of *up* with *in* will renew your powers for being right and doing right in a very short time.

So give in! *Give in to new energy and creative power!* This type of *giving in* was a personality power of all our great creative thinkers: Shakespeare, Benjamin Franklin, Abraham Lincoln, Thomas Edison, and a host of notable women. You see, *giving in* always *expands* your individuality, never surrenders it.

YOU DISCOVER YOUR NEW POWERS WHEN YOU GIVE IN TO THE POWERFUL LAWS OF LIFE

You can give in to the Laws of Life and so draw your needed powers by speaking a language that combines an eagerness for success with a stout belief in success. So that you will have an exact idea of power-packed phrases to use, read and review these examples:

"I give in to those inner strengths which will enable me to give out new powers for creative energy."

"I expect progress; I know no direction but forward."

"Even when confused or disappointed, I am still on my way."

"I welcome life-challenges as healthy exercises in life-growth."

"I learn something from everything."

"I never permit fear or pride to stand in the way of finding and using my untapped resources."

LET YOUR WORDS DO THE WORK!

Instructors in auto-driving schools frequently advise student drivers, "Let the car do the work. There's plenty of power under that hood. All you need to do is master it. Don't strain yourself, simply use your hands and eyes to *direct* the power. The car will obey your every command. Be the director; let the car do the work."

You will be doing a clever and effective thing when you apply this idea to the powers of your speech. In other words, let the words do the work. You already know the mighty force that is released from the tip of your tongue every time you speak, so have confidence that your phrases will accomplish the task you have set for them. Every time you speak in a dauntless manner, know that you have given the proper directions, realize that the power you have set in action will now act for your benefit. Understand that high speech puts you into high gear. Now since this is so, you have no reason for straining or wearing yourself out. All you need to do is sit back, give commands, and enjoy the ride.

TALK YOURSELF FORWARD . . . STAY OUT OF REVERSE

When I suggested this "high verbal gear" to a friend he told me, "It was just what I needed to save me from useless strain. I'm always at ease in the driver's seat!"

If you are straining on the hills or perilously careening around sharp bends, I suggest you also sit back and let your words carry you safely forward. Imagine positive speech as the forward gear in your car-of-life, negative speech as the reverse gear. Then express forward-moving phrases, no matter how high the hills or sharp the curves. Keep yourself in high gear with high speech. Shift gears when necessary; if you find yourself slipping back, slip once more into high verbal gear.

TURN YOUR FREE MOMENTS TO ADVANTAGE

No doubt you have heard philosophical statements to the effect that we become that which we constantly think about. It is also a scientifically proven fact. We *do* develop characteristics and abilities after our secret thoughts. Says Professor

Overstreet: "You are, in short, that to which you habitually attend."[1] You can gather your own happy proof by playing the following word-game as you drive the highway or go about your daily affairs. Try to think of all the synonyms possible for certain energizing words. For *energy* you might come up with *vigor, strength, power, zest, vitality.* For *success* you could supply *achievement, triumph, prosperity, victory, accomplishment.*

Now claim them to be true of yourself. Little by little your inner speakings will evidence themselves in outward gain.

A FEW WORDS ABOUT ANGRY WORDS

That our words have creative power is experimentally proven by us every day. And nothing is more certain than that angry words create life-limiting emotional states. For instance, have you ever spoken in an irritating manner while feeling peaceful about it? No. Ever utter anxious words while feeling secure? Impossible. Speaking in wrath, pride, and envy is the sure way to exist in a similar state.

Try blowing your breath and swallowing at the same time and you will see how equally impossible it is to blow angry words and swallow energizing peace.

I mention this to give you additional motivation for practicing all the techniques in this book which will enable you to arrive at that powerful state where it is impossible for you to speak anything but creative words. When you reach this superior mental state you will be able to say something similar to these words of Epictetus:

"Reckon the days in which you have not been angry: I used to be angry every day; now every other day; then every third and fourth day; and if you miss it so long as thirty days, offer a sacrifice of thanksgiving to God."

You see, if one man can achieve, so can the man that is you. Try as you will, you cannot think of a God who would play favorites when handing out good gifts. "Put off . . . the former

[1] H. A. Overstreet, *Influencing Human Behavior* (New York: W. W. Norton & Company, Inc., 1925).

conversation . . . and be renewed in the spirit of your mind." (Ephesians 4:22, 23) This is your logical starting point to make things end as you wish.

"THE WORDS OF THE WISE ARE AS . . . NAILS"

We have used many illustrations in this book to describe the ways in which our words can build us up or tear us down. Let's think of them now as the nails with which we build and secure our dream castles.

Now nails that are bent or broken can only promote careless, uncomfortable construction which is at the mercy of every passing storm. Perhaps you know people who are futilely hammering away, desperately trying to build their lives with nails of complaint, cynicism, worry. Take the bitter individual who vents his feelings of inferiority by running down successful folks. He wastes the very verbal energies that could easily be turned into a power for his own success. One look tells you he is trying to dwell in security where there can be no security, for he is violating basic psychological laws.

But you also know folks whose lives are firmly held together with bright, shiny nails that fit just right. They live comfortably, assuredly, gently. Like Noah of old, who constructed his ark after the loving words of God, they always find themselves at rest, regardless of the raging storms outside.

As I write this I am reminded of one of these restful persons, a physically handicapped gentleman who calls from his front porch to his passing neighbors, "Wait a minute! I have good news for you!" The good news is always welcomed for it consists of humorous stories or sincere compliments on the neighbor's attractive garden or a word of appreciation for the neighbor's kindness. Were you to ask him why he is so eager to report good news I imagine he would reply, "Because cheery words make cheery faces—theirs and mine!"

You too can gain the advantage that these restful folks enjoy. You too can be at daily ease by becoming a wise master of your daily expressions. Take this as your blueprint: "The words of the wise are as . . . nails fastened by the masters of assemblies." (Ecclesiastes 12:11)

BUILD YOUR DREAM CASTLES WITH CONSTRUCTIVE WORD-NAILS

I suggested a physical exercise to a disillusioned acquaintance by asking him to actually take two small buckets and fill one with twisted nails and the other with new ones. "Ask yourself which type you wish to build with," I told him, "and every evening take a single nail from the bucket that represents your dominant speech habit for the day. Place whichever type it may be upon the pictures of homes—one an unattractive shack and the other a lovely castle. Now build with word-nails that will contribute only to the castle."

After several days he remarked, "I've got the idea! I've been pounding away my energies. From now on I'm building a new, invigorating life for myself!"

You can also become a master assembler of your life castles by nailing yourself together with nails from the right pails.

TRY THE "I PREFER" TECHNIQUE

Whenever you are bothered by anything at all, whenever you feel low in spirits and high in tensions, tell yourself that you prefer to feel otherwise. Don't try to force anything, don't wonder whether you have enough faith to see it through; simply inform your feelings that you choose an opposite state. Authoritatively announce something like, "I prefer energy, an exuberant spirit. I perfer hopeful and expectant attitudes. I prefer believing that good things are mine."

Now do something that will further promote your preferences. Talk cheerfully to someone, play a rousing game, do anything that will permit you to forget yourself for a while. Perhaps without realizing it you will feel exactly as you choose to feel. The voluntary act of getting outside of yourself is a sure-fire means of getting to know your superior self.

A college football player was having trouble hanging onto

the forward passes tossed his way. His coach shouted, "Get out of yourself and into the game!" The player caught onto the idea that his jittery self-concern was translating itself into physical awkwardness. As soon as he unfroze his tense state of mind by getting whole-heartedly into the game he caught the ball every time. In much the same way we can induce high spirits by getting out of ourselves and entering whole-heartedly into the game of life.

For simplicity and clarity there is no better summary than the wisdom of Epictetus: "First say to yourself what you would be; and then do what you have to do."

LIVELY SUGGESTIONS FOR LIVELY LIVING

1. Know that a fired-up enthusiasm can light your way to whatever goal you choose . . . and know that you can have the necessary enthusiasm.

2. To cast weariness and boredom from your life, broadcast only cheery verbal programs.

3. Become aware of and absorb the abundant goodness that surrounds you at the present moment. Calmly accept your riches now.

4. See yourself—and express yourself—as gracefully hurdling all barriers.

5. Make your wealthy self visible with wealthy words!

6. Give in to your inner powers—and you will give out a power-packed personality.

7. Talk yourself forward. Relax in the sure knowledge that your words are working for you.

8. Use your spare moments to impress yourself with verbal vitalities. Connect success words with a successful self.

9. Build your dream castles with nails from the right pails!

10. Tell yourself what you prefer, then prefer to believe in your victory.

WORDS OF LOVE — FOR A LIFE FULL OF LOVE

Chapter 11

IT IS TRUE THAT LOVE IS WHAT MAKES the world go around. But most folks want to spin more gloriously dizzy.

There are so many magnificent things that true love will do for you: Love will fill you with vitality and enthusiasm for life . . . infuse you with new dreams and give you the power to make them come true . . . set you free from anger, loneliness, frustration . . . banish struggle and weariness . . . constantly delight, refresh, and surprise you . . . carry you lightly and loftily through life . . . and make you truly happy.

Victor Hugo sums up, "The supreme happiness of life is the conviction that we are loved."

It follows that the supreme agony is the conviction (an unnecessary one) that we are neither loved nor loving.

THE GREATEST TALENT YOU WILL EVER POSSESS IS THE TALENT FOR LOVING

All else is secondary. "First things first" is the wise proverb. Love is first. Put it first and perhaps for the first time in your life you will be free from every unloving thing in your life.

Love is a talent. Yes, a talent, just as one might have a talent for playing the piano or for growing roses.

FURTHERMORE, LOVE IS A TALENT OF WHICH YOU ARE FULLY CAPABLE

Perhaps you cannot play the piano or grow roses, but if you have a heart at all you have one that can be filled with joy-giving love. You have a present *capacity* for love, regardless of any present emptiness.

The human heart is like a perfume bottle. It is meant to be filled with sweetness. Even when empty, the capacity for fullness remains. You are the perfume-maker who can fill it with the sweet scent of a loving life.

The beauty of the heart is that it aspires to beauty. Keep this idea foremost in your thinking and it will prove to be a marvelous love-promoter. ***The beauty of the heart is that it aspires to beauty.***

YOU HAVE A DEEP DESIRE FOR LOVE

The essential element for developing any talent is *desire*. You now have this desire for love. Everyone has. Even those who cannot or will not admit it. It is always a deep yearning, perhaps not outwardly expressed but always inwardly longing to manifest itself.

Says Ashley Montagu: "The greatest of all needs of the human being is the need for love, the experiencing of the feeling conveyed by 'others' that one is wanted, needed, liked, appreciated, valued, and deeply involved with the 'other' or 'others.' "[1]

This chapter will supply you with practical pointers for fully manifesting your talents for love, affection, tenderness—which, incidentally, will be returned to you because there is no such thing as unreturned love; love is both the Giver and the Gift.

These principles are applicable to romantic love, love for friends, love whatever, for true love embraces everyone and everything. Love is always a way of life.

[1] Ashley Montagu, ed., *The Meaning of Love* (New York: The Julian Press, Inc., 1953).

ALL POSITIVE SPEECH IS LOVING SPEECH

First of all, understand that all types of positive speech are life-loving speech. Expressions of faith and hope, poise and confidence, phrases filled with determination and cheeriness are signs of love in the one who expresses them.

Keep this idea in mind as you practice your affirmations. Know that loving words create loving natures. Understand that the ultimate purpose in speaking beautiful words is to live them out in your life.

TELL YOURSELF ALL THE REASONS WHY YOU CAN LOVE

For every shallow reason the world may give you for not living the tranquil, affectionate life, you can give yourself a thousand wisdom-wealthy reasons why you *can.* I suggest you duplicate the word-power method used by a Pennsylvania woman for getting her heart and mind into a receptive mood. She wrote down all the reasons why she could love:

"I can love because . . . my eyes can *see* love, my ears can *hear* love, my lips can *speak* love, my mind can *believe* love, my heart can *feel* love, my emotions can *express* love, my attitudes can *manifest* love, my hands can *act* love, my life can *live* love."

"I LOVE"

Stop your reading at this very moment to quietly affirm, "I love." Say it with a relaxed sigh. Now forget it. Go back to the book. Don't think about it for a while. Reason: If you stop to think at this point you may also stop to doubt. At all costs you must not permit the entrance of doubtful, negative emotions.

An hour or two later again affirm with all the conviction possible, "I love." Make it a general, simple statement of fact. Again forget it. Go about your business. If doubts arise, reject them as false, dismiss them with the contrary affirmation of, "I love."

Continue to do this several times a day, perhaps ten or twelve times during a 24-hour period. To repeat, it is vital that you do not mentally struggle with your words, "I love." Simply plant the seed, refuse to dig it up with doubts, and let it grow of itself.

During the following days expand your expression. Do it by directing it toward whatever you desire to love. But be sure to put the emphasis on the fact that *you* love, not that you love *this* or *that*. Love is always *you*, not a person or an object. *You* love.

WHAT WILL HAPPEN?

Perhaps this seems too simple, too abrupt. You probably want to know what will happen. This elementary technique will become clearer to you as you proceed with the chapter. Just patiently, persistently try it. The wonderful results will be your best evidence as to its power. Don't let a lack of full understanding hold you back. You need never venture very far into the night to see your first star.

As an example of this, an Indiana woman patiently practices what she calls "Love Assignments." Her practice consists of deliberately assigning enjoyable qualities to everyone, regardless of how ill-suited they seem to be, and equally important, in spite of her own meager grasp of the process involved. She says, "This technique not only returns to me a deep sense of fulfillment but it has a way of enabling these loved folks to live up to their assignments. I guess this is because when people sense that they are loved they find it easy to love in return."

Believe this: It is much better to say that *you love* and not be sure of what you are saying, than to say that *you don't love* and know what you are talking about!

"GO IN THE WAY OF UNDERSTANDING"

Folks who seek a more loving way of life are usually advised to get an understanding of love, to gain a deeper insight into their relationship with it, to rid themselves of anxieties and suspicions.

Perfect advice. But it leaves most folks with the age-old question, "How can a man . . . understand his own way?" (Proverbs 20:24)

I would like to tell you a story that will further show you how to "Go in the way of understanding." (Proverbs 9:6)

WHEN YOU SEEK THE KINGDOM OF LOVE...

In the romantic days of King Arthur there once lived a brave and sincere knight named Sir Seeker. "I seek the Kingdom of Love," he humbly proclaimed as he stood before King Arthur. "See! I have made ready my Sword of Attack and my Shield of Defense!"

"Sincere knight," replied gentle King Arthur, "to find the Kingdom of Love you must venture forth with neither your Sword of Attack nor Shield of Defense. The Kingdom of Love is found only by the brave knight who neither attacks nor defends himself."

"But is this not unusual?" questioned Sir Seeker. "I have won other great kingdoms with my sharp sword and stout armor."

"That is why you have found only the Kingdom of Fame and the Kingdom of Wealth," observed the king. "But Love is a Kingdom that is found only by those who refuse to struggle. Go, Sir Seeker, bravely venture down the Road of Understanding without weapons of any kind and you will find the wonderful Kingdom you so earnestly seek."

No sooner was Sir Seeker outside the castle walls than he was attacked by the Dragon of Doubt. "Halt!" screamed the fire-breathing monster. "Because of me you cannot proceed. My fiery breath will turn you back!"

DECLARATIONS OF FAITH WILL LEAVE DOUBT FAR BEHIND

But having no weapons with which to either attack or retreat, Sir Seeker firmly replied, "Nothing—not even the Dragon of Doubt—can turn me from the Kingdom of Love. I refuse all your doubtful suggestions."

With this heroic declaration he left a doubtful-looking Dragon of Doubt far behind as he advanced along the Road of Understanding.

A few hours later he was abruptly accosted by the Black Knight of Heartbreak. "Hah!" gleefully shouted the Black Knight as he furiously charged down the Road. "I will spill you off the Road of Understanding. I am a very dark and powerful influence in your life. I have broken your heart in the past and I will do it again!"

Neither attacking nor retreating, Sir Seeker simply rode forward. As the Black Knight of Heartbreak rushed harmlessly past, Sir Seeker shouted, "Once and for all I reject your attacks on me. I steadily ride on to the Kingdom of Love in spite of your foolish threats."

With this cry of victory he easily rode down the Road of Understanding, leaving the Black Knight of Heartbreak with a broken heart at having his bluff called.

Later that day the Sorceress of Complaint slinkily stepped before him. "Come with me to my Kingdom of Complaint," she slyly invited, "and we will go complainingly through life together. You'll be amazed at all the wonderful things we can complain about. Not only that but the Kingdom of Complaint is an excellent place to prepare for the Kingdom of Bitterness and the Kingdom of Depression."

HAVE NOTHING TO DO WITH COMPLAINT

Not taking the trouble to either attack or retreat before the vicious invitation, Sir Seeker courageously replied, "I will have none of you and your disastrous kingdoms. You will not rob me of the wonderful Kingdom of Love."

With this exclamation he proceeded down the Road of Understanding, leaving the Sorceress of Complaint to mutter bitter complaints.

During the next few days he happily and effortlessly passed the Forest of Fear, the Peak of Pride, and the Desert of Dejection.

"What an unusual but glorious Road is the Road of Understanding," he reflected as he rode on. "To make good progress one needs the unique Power of powerlessness."

When he finally reached the end of the Road of Understanding he was surprised to find himself back in King Arthur's kingdom.

"What is this?" he asked in happy amazement. "I have returned to where I started. Is *this* the Kingdom of Love?"

LOVE IS WHEREVER YOU ARE

"The Kingdom of Love is wherever you are," explained King Arthur, "as long as you stand at the end of the Road of Understanding. You have boldly traveled the Road without attacking or retreating. So, sincere Sir Seeker, fully enter into your enjoyment of the Kingdom of Love."

A fine example of this courageous forward drive was described in a religious magazine in which a woman confessed her sunken state of disappointment and depression. But by imprinting the self-propelling words, "Forgetting those things which are behind, and reaching forth unto those things which are before," (Philippians 3:13) she gained a rich understanding of Christ's declaration that the kingdom of God was within. By firmly holding onto the truth that God had willed her a life-legacy of "growing and glowing" (as she put it) she found the kingdom of love wherever she happened to be at the moment, for God's love was eternally within her. "No longer was I depressed," she concluded, "for my understanding of God's lovely world truly made it a lovely world."

TAKE THE "IN SPITE OF" ATTITUDE

Nothing in the world can prevent you from finding your own Kingdom of Love if you will maintain the "in spite of" frame of mind, if you will firmly stand up and speak up to those roadside "enemies." In spite of past heartache, in spite of present threats, in spite of future apprehensions, you will arrive if you will but proceed in spite of them all. If you have been fighting and falling (and you have been falling if you are unhappy) know that love's secrets are revealed to those who patiently and quietly seek them out . . . and speak them out.

Your Road of Understanding will become easier, happier, brighter as you refuse to verbally fight your fears (false fears) or retreat before your doubts. Folks who dwell in the Kingdom of Love will tell you that the journey itself is a refreshing, invigorating challenge. You can have the same refreshing experience if you will easily, almost casually, proceed to the end of the Road of Understanding. So do it in spite of everything. You don't want to miss it for anything!

YOU ALWAYS **ATTRACT** WHAT YOU **ARE.** ARE YOU LOVING?

The quiet but desperate cry of the human heart is, "I want to attract love. I want someone to tell me that I am loved. I want to tell someone that I love him. More than anything else in the world I want love . . . but where in the world do I find it?"

You have previously read this all-important principle: *You always attract what you are.* (And remember, you are what you *believe* you are.)

It is useless and heart-breaking to try to attract anything that is not first a part of your own self.

You do not *find* love . . . you *live* love.

To *have* a loving state you must first *be* in a loving state.

You do not fall in love because you meet a loving woman; you meet a loving woman because you are a loving man.

There is no greater personal tragedy than the person who is incapable of knowing love from another because he or she has an unloving self. The most beautiful lady on earth must listen in dreadful incomprehension to a man's love-lyrics if she herself knows not the meaning of love.

To understand the language of love you must also be able to speak the same language.

There is no other way . . . no other *magical* way, for once you master the language of love you need never again cry out in a desperate tongue. Rather, you easily draw to you those who understand and are understood.

WRITE LOVE LETTERS

If you want to create a love-consciousness within yourself you can do so by using your word power in this manner: Create a number of lofty, gracious words, each containing a different number of letters, for example: three letters, *joy;* four letters, *care;* five letters, *peace;* six letters, *friend;* seven letters, *harmony;* eight letters, *devotion;* nine letters, *abundance;* ten letters, *heartiness.*

Think of as many of these pleasant words as you can. Write them down. Think of what they mean; think of what they mean to *you.* Visualize and meditate upon physical objects that the words represent, such as a good friend or an abundant orchard. This act of deliberately concentrating your attention on loftiness will prove to be a self-enriching occupation.

CONCENTRATE ON BEING LOVING . . . LOVE WILL DO THE REST

Set aside, for the time, that which you *want* from love. Concentrate on what you will *become* in love. Concern yourself with loving words and you will become their likeness. Absolutely, this will give you what you want.

A wandering alcoholic, separated from his wife and family for three years, regained his place in life by pursuing this tremendous truth. After recovering his sobriety in a "last resort" rescue mission he pitifully sobbed to a mission worker, "I want my wife to love me as she used to. Will you write her a letter? . . . tell her how much I need her?"

"Who caused her present attitude toward you?" he was asked.

"I did, of course."

"Then who has the responsibility for changing her feelings toward you?"

"Myself," he thoughtfully replied.

"Then who has to get busy?"

With a glimmer of understanding of his own duty toward his wife's feelings he repeated, "Myself."

This clarified idea of his duty supplied him with enough prodding to accept professional help. In due time his self-respect and self-command returned—and his wife was only too eager to give him the love he wanted. In once more *becoming* a lovable man he *received* what he became.

TO BE IN LOVE, **BELIEVE** IN LOVE

Love never happens. In one way or another it is always planned by you. This is not only a philosophical precept but a Law of Life you daily reflect. Your attitudes and beliefs toward love determine the plan that works out in your life for either joy or bitterness. Why, the homeliest man on earth may well be loved by a woman who believes him the handsomest. He has the happy responsibility for perpetuating her faith by living as a handsome man. It makes absolutely no difference whether his physical appearance conforms or not: their mutually handsome plan is always a loving reality, for love sees not the face but its grace.

Believe in love. Know that it is a reality. Be thankful for it. Praise it. Believe that it is yours. Personalize it. Speak words of love; speak in love and of love. Love will then echo your words of belief.

Resolve with Browning, "I will speak thy speech, Love."

HOW YOU CAN BELIEVE IN LOVE

If love baffles and eludes you, I want to give you a word-power method that will clear up your thinking and create the tender way of life. It's the easy way.

Take a sheet of paper. Give it the heading, WHAT I PRESENTLY BELIEVE ABOUT LOVE. Now frankly list all your presently felt beliefs of a negative nature, perhaps something like this:

"I am cynical about love."

"It is found only in fiction."

"Love is a gamble."

"It means too much sacrifice."

"I can get along without love."

Completely exhaust your innermost feelings. Don't be afraid to face your opinions, for you are keeping your list in secret.

CORRECTLY DEFINE LOVE

Next, take another sheet and head it, WHAT I *WANT* TO BELIEVE ABOUT LOVE. Now write down those positive words which express your ideals of love. Define love as it would exist to your full satisfaction. Be just as boldly honest as before. Something like this:

"I believe in love."

"Love is mine."

"Love is peaceful, steady, reliable."

"Giving of my love results in my receiving of love."

"Needing love, I courageously seek its fullness."

You now have two contradictory lists. It so happens that the first list is false, the second is good and true. *It is good and true whether or not you have personally experienced it as good and true.*

MAKE LOVE COME TRUE FOR YOU

Isn't it nicely coincidental that what you *want* to believe is also what is true? . . . even though you may not have experienced it as yet?

Here is how to make love come true: Tear up the first sheet. Toss it away. As the pieces slip from your fingers say to yourself, "Negativity is gone forever. No more cynicism, no false beliefs. I was weary of them anyway."

Take the second sheet. Read it. Read it over and over. Live with it. Express thoughts and words that amplify your new belief. Remind yourself that what you want to believe is also what you *do* believe. Get independent. Exclaim, "I'm going to do what I want to do."

Your very desire to accept your new definitions will take you far. Make no mistake, the desire will always be there, so feed it constantly with loving phrases.

LOVE IS AT YOUR REQUEST

When this plan was suggested to a saleswoman whose job required dealings with "difficult people" she came back with the question, "But what if I find myself out of control? Difficult people are really *difficult*. I think I need more help."

"Request your arm to rise above your head," she was instructed.

Her arm rose high above her head.

"Request your face to smile," the instructor said.

She gave forth with a lovely smile.

"Your body obeys your mental commands, doesn't it?" he said. "As a baby you had trouble controlling the expressions of your arms and face but as you grew in self-command you also grew in self-control."

She pondered his point. "You mean I can also learn to request proper emotions?"

"In much the same way. Know that you have a God-given intellect that has power over your feelings. Think of yourself as the sole authority over yourself. Do not permit your negativity to impose upon you. Continually request your inner love to manifest itself and it will certainly do so."

In a matter of days she found herself calmly handling her difficult people. Her requested composure more and more revealed itself.

If you will do likewise, if you will request your love to rise above and beyond your present self, you will also make your love come true. So request it . . . and rest in it.

UNDERSTAND THAT TRUE LOVE IS A COURAGEOUS, RELAXED, GENTLE POWER

Love is always gently courageous. Love is, in a sense, a synonym of relaxed heroism. Love is a free, outgiving, easy flow of power.

Love never asks nor cares whether it will be accepted or rejected. It never knows fear, it knows only itself. The loving man or woman can no more help but express love than the rain can help but shower in abandoned blessing on its world.

It is this valorous shower of love that is capable of creating rainbows.

You can create more rainbows in your life by reading and meditating on these loving thoughts which describe love as it truly is:

LOVE IS MANY LOVELY THINGS

Love is a song . . . cheery.
Love is a silence . . . tranquil.

Love is a garden . . . secluded.
Love is a meadow . . . expansive.

Love is a mountain . . . towering.
Love is a valley . . . humble.

Love is a dawn . . . refreshing.
Love is a twilight . . . restful.

Love is a kiss . . . tender.
Love is a handclasp . . . firm.

Love is a shade . . . cooling.
Love is a sun . . . warming.

Love is a boy . . . eager.
Love is a girl . . . airy.

Love is a sail . . . yielding.
Love is a rudder . . . guiding.

Love is a sigh . . . relaxing.
Love is a gasp . . . delighting.

Love is a hand . . . giving.
Love is a palm . . . receiving.

PATRICIA AND GARY HAVE A LOVE INCIDENT

Patricia and Gary were two nice people but they didn't get along so nicely. The first thing they did as they sat before a counsellor was to express their bewilderment.

"We can't figure it out," they said. "We go happily along for a few days and *bang* . . . everything explodes between us. We *want* to get along but . . ."

"What usually sets things off?" asked the counsellor.

Gary frowned. "That's just it. It's almost always a little thing of no importance. She makes a remark that I don't like or I do something that upsets her. If we could just control these foolish quarrels over trivial matters . . ."

"I can give you a workable technique for building peace and harmony into your everyday affairs," the counsellor assured them, "but both of you must agree to see it through."

DISMISS THE INCIDENT

When they sincerely agreed, the counsellor continued: "The very next time an incident occurs I want you to immediately dismiss every thought connected with it. Forget it. Pretend it didn't happen, for though you may not be aware of it, the incident is not the problem at all."

They agreed to dismiss the incident from their thinking.

AFFIRM YOUR LOVE

"Gary," the counsellor went on, "your next step is to quietly say to yourself, 'I love Patricia and she loves me. That's it, that's final. I dearly love her and she dearly loves me.' And Patricia, you do the same."

"We really *do* care for each other," Patricia spoke up.

"Of course you do. I want you to fully understand that these little incidents turn into big upsets because each of you feels under personal attack from the other. Your self-esteem is threatened. When that happens you temporarily abandon your belief in the other's love. This false belief that the other has withdrawn his love causes you to strike out in bitterness and injured pride. You then draw icily back, you fearfully withdraw to avoid further hurt."

"Is *that* what is actually at the bottom of our hostility?" asked Gary. "We temporarily doubt our love?"

REJECT BASELESS INSECURITY

"Exactly. You permit a false sense of insecurity to enter. The next thing I want you to do is to ruthlessly toss it out."

"Let's make sure we get this," said Gary as he counted off on his fingers. "First of all, forget the incident. Second, assure myself of her love. Third, reject all false feelings of insecurity."

Their counsellor nodded. "Reject those painful feelings by declaring, 'I refuse to believe that I am under personal attack. I reject the idea. Pride costs too much. I will have none of it. I love her and she loves me.' "

Patricia smiled. "This is something new. It sounds great."

STEP VALIANTLY FORWARD, SPEAK UP

"Your self-spoken words have now put you in a powerful position to take the final and most important step of all. I want one of you—it makes no difference which, but Gary I think it would be nice if you take the lead—to simply walk over and speak to Patricia. Make any casual comment that has nothing to do with the incident. Ask her if she wants some coffee, tell her that you'll make it. And Patricia, you will reply that you'd love some coffee and thanks for making it."

Gary smiled at the picture. "I see. We have now reassured each other. It's a subtle way of saying, 'I love you.' "

HUMILITY IS LOVE-IN-ACTION

"Remember above all," the counsellor emphasized, "that whoever takes the first step toward the other is displaying great strength of character. It takes lots of love-power to take that first step. Humility is always strength, never weakness."

"AN AMAZING THING WILL HAPPEN . . ."

"An amazing thing will happen when you persist in believing in each other. Those little incidents will occur less and less as you both gain a fuller confidence in each other's love and esteem. You will be delighted to find that the very things that now upset you have no ability at all to cause distress. It's all a matter of self-esteem. Once you know you are loved, nothing else seems to matter. You will probably have some good chuckles over those previously disturbing incidents. Finally, let me emphasize that it is all-important that *you proceed in spite of any skepticism you may encounter from your own mind or the other.* Skepticism will be natural to both of you at the start, but it will gradually fall away as you see practical results."

At a later conference Gary and Patricia reported gratifying success. They were overjoyed to find that once the first bold step was taken in the direction of the other that everything else seemed trivial. The problem was easily solved or dismissed as unimportant.

DO THE OPPOSITE!

This technique will be equally successful in your life, for it is based on a fundamental truth. That truth is: *When you speak and do the opposite of what you usually speak and do, results are also of an opposite nature.*

So do the opposite of what you usually do when love seems threatened. Forget the problem; kick it out, don't kick it around. Assure yourself of the other's love. Refuse to believe in feelings of love-lack. Take that first bold and humble step toward the other. Say, "I love you." Follow Shakespeare's advice: "Speak low, if you speak love."

Besides all this, men should realize that women are so easily reassured. The next time your wife awakens you at three in the morning to ask whether you still love her, just sleepily mutter "Umph" while gently kicking her in the shins. She will peacefully turn over and dream of you as the world's greatest lover.

EVERYTHING ELSE BECOMES EASY

It is not at all an oversimplification to say that courageous love itself will solve the problem or banish the incident. What a lack of confidence in love created as a distress, a stout belief in love will overcome.

When you think love, speak love, act love, there can be no hardship. The human heart's first need is for tender love . . . when filled with tender love it makes everything else easy.

SWEETEN YOUR LIFE WITH THIS SUMMARY

1. Affirm your talent for love and affection, affirm the love of others.

2. Quietly insist that a fuller, richer love-life can be yours.

3. Patiently go down the Road of Understanding, ignore temptations to turn aside. Proceed in spite of everything.

4. Concentrate on being loving . . . and you will surely draw the love you want.

5. Believe in love as the good and true power that it is. Define it only as you wish it to be to you.

6. Make love come true by following all the suggested steps.

7. Impress yourself with the truth that love is always gently heroic.

8. Know that love rushes in to fill the vacuum left by vanishing fears.

9. Realize that humble approaches are love-in-action.

10. Practice the "do the opposite" technique . . . and everything else becomes easy.

BE POPULAR, WIN FRIENDS, BANISH LONELINESS THROUGH WORD POWER

Chapter 12

I KNOW ALL THE RULES FOR ACQUIRING a popular personality and for winning friends," said Leonard D., "for I have read dozens of books on the subject. I know that I must be kind and considerate, I realize I must see the other fellow's viewpoint, I am aware that to have a friend I must be a friend. But," he gloomily added, "I'm right where I started. My friendly approaches seem to have a way of getting fouled up. I just can't draw close to people, I just can't get them to understand me. I'm beginning to think those book-rules are a bunch of nothings that have no practical meaning."

"The rules are fundamentally right," his advisor told him, "it is your wrong mental attitude that causes you to miss."

Leonard sighed. "I knew you'd say that. But go ahead, get specific, tell me exactly what I must do."

"You need to observe but two golden rules when applying the friendship fundamentals. First, forget what effect your words and deeds will have on others. Second, concentrate on what effect they will have on you."

Leonard squinted in doubt and bewilderment. "But that sounds all wrong. I *want* to have an effect on others; as a matter of fact that's the whole idea. Besides, it sounds selfish to think of myself, to put myself first."

YOU ARE THE MAGNET

"Leonard, listen very carefully." His advisor held up a forefinger to emphasize his point. "The only way you can ever arrive at the place where you can freely give others the kindness they wish is for you yourself to be in a kindly position. It is you, it is your subconscious attitudes which must first be changed to kindness and consideration. If you will concentrate on making yourself right you will be surprised at the powers you will possess for making right relationships."

"Go on."

"Think of yourself as a magnet," the advisor continued. "Tell me, as a boy did you ever run a toy magnet through the earth in order to attract bits of iron?"

"Yes."

"It was always the magnet that counted, wasn't it? As long as it was charged with power it easily drew those bits of iron wherever it was placed."

"That's right."

"Likewise, you need only concern yourself with charging your personality with magnetic qualities. Once you are attractive you will not be able to keep folks from eagerly moving themselves toward you. You will pick up attractive friends wherever you go."

Leonard mused, "That's a surprising twist. I should direct my attention toward the effect that my friendly gestures are having on my own attitudes, rather than on the folks concerned."

"Yes. When you approach it from this new angle an interesting thing will happen. You will find yourself thinking less and less of yourself and more and more of how you can give of your good self to others. As strange as it now sounds, it is only when you first put yourself first that you are eventually enabled to put others first. It is the right, the honorable, and unselfish way. It is the only way that will result in all-around happiness."

During the following weeks Leonard D. pictured himself as an attractive magnet that was more and more charged with power as he practiced his friendship fundamentals. He directed his attention toward the wonderful effect his kindly words and deeds had on his own emotions and attitudes. In one instance, after complimenting his wife on an excellent dinner, he took an inside look to observe his own emotional reaction—to discover that he felt just as good about it as did his wife! He made the mental note that sincere compliments cannot be paid to others without a corresponding complimentary feeling returning to himself. *His* compliment was *his* reward. So the more the merrier, he concluded.

Another time he spent an hour quietly listening to the troubles of a friend. Again he observed that his patient role opened to him new feelings of sympathy and understanding—which were *his* personal riches.

After continuing with self-observation for a while he found that several bright things had happened: *(a)* He was more free from self-centered feelings, thus at liberty to further enrich himself by giving more. *(b)* He was happier, increasingly self-satisfied. *(c)* He was really appreciating and enjoying others. *(d)* Others were really appreciating and enjoying *him!*

This fine idea can be summed up with:

Watch the rewards that come your way when you are friendly toward others, and in proportion to your creation of your rewards you will be able to forget yourself—and cause others to remember you!

YOU HAVE THE POWER TO MAKE PEOPLE THE WAY YOU WISH THEM TO BE!

One of the most delightful discoveries you will ever make is that you can infuse others with those friendly, gentle characteristics that you wish to have returned to you. The only condition for attaining this refined power is to first *make yourself what you should be to yourself.* Says Goethe, "If you would create something you must *be* something." The creator must be equal to his desired creation.

You see, it is only when you are truly pleased with yourself that you can please others. "Love thy neighbour as thyself," (Mark 12:31) is the true way. But in order to love another human being you must first have a healthy love for the human being that is yourself. The self-satisfied and happy individual is the only one who has the ability to distribute happiness. You can only give that which you have. The law of Give and Take can only be set in motion by a Giver. You should rejoice in the wonderful news that a Giver is automatically a Receiver.

TAKE A DEEP SIGH OF RELIEF AT THIS GOOD NEWS

Want to feel a tremendous relief at this very moment? Take a deep sigh as you impress yourself with: "I will first put myself first in all my dealings with others. I understand that the only thing I have to give is a portion of my own loving self; I will therefore put my loving self forward more and more. What a delightful relief to realize that this is the only right and rewarding way."

I have no doubt that you are tremendously relieved, for somewhere deep inside you have always wanted to put yourself first but you didn't know exactly how to do it. I have no doubt but that you now like yourself much better and that you are now able to truly express your liking for others. Without doubt you are on your way toward enjoying people rather than enduring them.

DO THIS:

1. Don't ask yourself what effect you are having on others. Pay attention to what effect your friendly words and deeds are having on yourself.

2. Know that selfishness and frustration result from *not* rightly putting yourself first, rather than from putting yourself first. Know that when you take proper care of yourself your friendships will naturally take care of themselves.

3. Proceed with your self-examination and positive speaking with the happy knowledge that this procedure will gradually give you a self-domination that will lead to the only kind of other-domination that brings mutual satisfaction—domination-in-love.

Now that this first principle is established, you can proceed to other ideas for building the affable life.

A TALE OF TWO BUNNIES

Once upon a meadow there lived two little bunny rabbits, one named Friendly Bunny and one named Friendless Bunny.

"What an unfriendly world," groaned Friendless Bunny as he crouched in his burrow. "The meadow is filled with people who hurt me most unkindly and who try to run my life for me and who try to gobble me up. Guess the only thing to do is crouch in the darkness and be miserable."

"Hop out and see a friend and you will have one," advised Friendly Bunny as he casually nibbled a carrot.

So Friendless Bunny cautiously hopped into the meadow but immediately scurried back with terror in his little pink eyes. "I saw a big wolf who tried to tear off my ears!" he screamed as he dove into the depths of his burrow. "Guess the only thing to do is sit in the dark and hate myself."

"Hop out and see a friend and you will have one," again advised Friendly Bunny.

So Friendless Bunny again ventured into the meadow but frantically flopped back into the burrow with the wail, "I saw a vicious fox who threatened to pull me apart. Guess the only thing to do is sit in the dark and hate everyone."

CORRECT YOUR VISION!

"I see that you are desperate," observed Friendly Bunny, "so I will give you my pair of Corrective Eye-Glasses. Here, wear them out into the meadow and see what you see."

Summoning his last ounce of courage Friendless Bunny put on the pair of Corrective Eye-Glasses and hesitantly poked his head out of the burrow.

"Look!" he happily shouted, "I see a friendly wolf!"

"That's the same unfriendly wolf you saw before," casually replied Friendly Bunny.

"And see!" Friendless Bunny joyously exclaimed, "I see the kindest-looking fox I ever saw in my life!"

"That's the very same vicious-looking fox you saw before," lazily commented Friendly Bunny.

Friendless Bunny ripped off the Corrective Eye-Glasses and called in sheer delight, "I now see friendly people *without* the glasses!"

"That's because you have corrected your vision," complimented Friendly Bunny. "Your next step is to hop-hop-hop toward those friendly folks you see-see-see."

"I see!" declared the new Friendly Bunny as he happily hopped into the meadow. "To *see* right is to *be* right!"

TRY THE "TOMATO TECHNIQUE"

Like to strike up some new friendships? Like to warm up the old ones? Do you wish a few additional folks around with whom you can share pleasant conversations and experiences? An Indiana woman did, and here's the amusing and practical way she did it:

"I knew that my outlook on life was all wrong. But I had just enough insight to realize that something could be done about it. Knowing that in order to *have* friends I had to *see* friends I devised my own word-power method for seeing friends wherever I went. I called it—don't laugh—the Tomato Technique. I gave it this name because I usually practiced it whenever I went shopping for groceries. While keeping one eye on my grocery list and the other on fellow shoppers I mentally spoke to myself:

"'I see a good friend over there by the tomatoes . . . and there's a friendly face in the next aisle . . . that woman with the baby-carriage is certainly likable . . . what a pleasant-looking man over there . . . there's another friend reaching for the bread . . . what a host of nice folks in the market . . .' and so on and on.

"Now of course these particular people did not become my friends; that wasn't the idea. The whole plan was to build a *friendship-consciousness* within myself, for believing in the eagerness of others to receive me and for convincing myself that I was an easy-going person who could contribute worth-while things to others.

"It worked! Not all at once, but as I gradually unfroze my inner warmths I magically saw changes take place in my social status. I actually experienced in real life what I had imaginatively declared to be my experiences. I had the very friendliness I had talked myself into believing."

SEE FRIENDS WHEREVER YOU GO

Talk yourself into the true view! Practice the right sight! Accept the world as accepting you. See friends wherever you go. *See* and you'll *be.*

Here is your perfect word-power declaration for accomplishing this:

"I behaved myself as though he had been my friend." (Psalm 35:14)

Some time ago the newspapers carried a story of a man who was told by a fortune-teller that he possessed something of "great value." Being somewhat gullible, he searched his attic with the idea that some old treasure might have been left there by his grandparents. Sure enough, he discovered himself the possessor of some valuable and long-forgotten postage stamps.

Not everyone has rare stamps in his attic but everyone possesses valuable and undiscovered treasures of love and grace. If you will now behave as if they are there, if you will be just "gullible" enough to believe that friendliness exists, you will put into motion a tremendous spiritual law—which no one fully understands but which anyone can apply—which will magnificently enrich your life. So seek them out until you find them and you will magically draw wonderful folks your way. The successful seeker eventually becomes the sought.

IF YOU ARE SENSITIVE, GOOD FOR YOU

"I'm a sensitive person," someone explains. "I'm touchy, my feelings are easily hurt. I'm quick to take offense to an unkind word or to getting neglected. When this happens I angrily withdraw. I know this is an unhealthy type of retreat, I know that this separates me from getting along with people but what else *can* I do when I get offended? My sensitivity is automatic, the only thing I know is retreat."

If you are easily offended, that's too bad . . . but I want you to know that this sensitivity of yours can be released in ways much too good for you to miss any longer.

First of all, realize that sensitivity can be a highly constructive characteristic. It means that you are alert, alive to life. Sensitivity is a requisite for writing a great symphony or for leading a vibrant life or for acquiring a popular personality.

IT ALL DEPENDS UPON YOUR USE OF YOUR POWERS OF SENSITIVITY

Your keen sense of feelings can either promote you in the world or push you into a frustrating corner of life. It depends upon what you do with it. So very much depends upon your correct use. You can either be gracefully sensitive as a flower or explosively sensitive as a bomb.

USE YOUR SPEECH TO TURN YOUR SENSITIVITY TOWARD THE LOVELY

You sometimes see printed lists of "the most beautiful words," such as *crystal, zephyr, bouquet.* The very reading of these lovely words induces sensitive emotions of a refreshing nature. You can apply this fine idea for inducing feelings of warmth and affection by creating your own list of "the most friendly words."

Think them up and write them down. Examples: *blossom, graceful, sparkle, sailing, caress, melody, inspire, esteem, dove, devotion, harmony, gift, pleasure.*

Now open your sensitivity to their lofty meanings. Make them a part of your everyday mental states. Speak them frequently. Insert them into your casual conversations. Associate them with your emotions. Let them surround and flow through you. Enjoy them whenever you speak or hear them. Live them.

A highly sensitive man devised this clever method for making this idea effective: "I pretended that the *only* words in the English language were gracious ones. Now since this was so, unfriendly or unpleasant words have absolutely no meaning to me, they just can't get through to my feelings. *Bitterness?* . . . never heard of it. But *idealism* . . . that's for me. *Inferiority?* . . . I don't know its meaning. But *power* . . . ah, I know full well the meaning of *that.*

"As I looked at the world through only rose-colored words I became rose-colored myself. I am relaxed, optimistic, unafraid of things that used to scare the wits out of me. I can honestly state that I am now sensitive only to the friendly. What a difference it makes in everything!"

YOUR WORDS ARE SENSITIVE FLASHES!

Picture your phrases as powerfully sensitive flashes of lightning. As lightning bolts link sky and earth, so your speech-flashes link you with the people in your world. Angry, fearful, envious words crash down with a destructive force, but speech charged with peace, kindness, and understanding lights up your world with a brilliance that dazzles and pleases. We have only slight control over natural lightning, but we can certainly master our highly charged flashes of speech.

**"The music that can deepest reach,
And cure all ill, is cordial speech."**

"I SOMETIMES GET SO LONELY . . ."

"I sometimes get so lonely I want to die."

Guess who used to say this. A hermit? A tester in a dynamite factory?

No. A woman who worked in an office with at least thirty fellow employees, a woman with a host of relatives and acquaintances, a woman who was always meeting new people.

Still, she was in honest agony when she groaned, "I sometimes get so lonely I want to die."

And she did die. A dozen times a day.

Why?

I'll tell you why.

Because she lived in a world of which she was not a part.

Why was she not a satisfying part of her world? The answer is so simple it's heartbreaking. Don't read another line of this book until it is perfectly clear to you. She was lonely because she pictured others as too busy or too disinterested or too critical to enjoy her. This frame of mind led her to believe that there was danger of rejection in trying to draw close to others. By wrongly picturing herself as alone she forced herself to mentally withdraw from people, thereby creating the very inner isolation she dreaded. In this self-made state she couldn't enjoy others, nor could others enjoy her.

In time, an advisor led her to see that others needed the riches of her life just as much as she needed theirs; therefore if she would mentally release herself she would both give and receive of riches. The advisor gave her some word magic that turned the trick: "Cease inner speakings of isolation. Verbally enter your world of people. Let them become interested in you as a human being possessed of both graces and faults. Show an interest in them as human beings possessed of the same. Step out and speak up and you will find joy and comfort, rather than danger, in drawing close to people."

DON'T BELIEVE IN LONELINESS, REJECT REJECTION AND YOU WILL NOT EXPERIENCE IT

If you are lonely, you are the lone creator of your loneliness. If this sounds harsh, we both know that loneliness is even harsher. If you will bravely face the truth that you are the creator of your own circumstances you are then in the wonderful position where you can create circumstances to your liking. It's worth pursuing, isn't it?

HERE IS WHAT YOU NEED:

A closeness. An intimacy. This is the yearning of the human heart. It is more than a host of friends that you really want and need. The young lady of the previous paragraphs was starving in the midst of plenty. It's the closeness. You want an intimacy, a sure knowledge that you belong, that you are necessary to someone. You need someone in whom you can confide, unburden your secret thoughts, with whom you can let go. You want someone who understands enough to accept you as you are; if they want to change you at all it is because they experience a loving intimacy with life that they wish to increasingly share with you.

You want the one Emerson describes, "A friend is a person with whom I may be sincere. Before him, I may think aloud."

You want Someone Special.

YOUR **SOMEONE SPECIAL** PRESENTLY EXISTS; HE OR SHE IS AS EAGER TO FIND YOU AS YOU ARE EAGER TO FIND HIM

This special person somewhere now exists for you. The only reason—you *must* believe this—that you may not have found him or her is because you do not believe that for everyone there is someone. But there surely is. It could be someone you now know, a casual acquaintance, or a stranger who has yet to make his appearance. God didn't stop when he made Eve for Adam.

WHAT CAN YOU DO ABOUT IT? DO THIS:

Use the various word-power procedures described in this book for turning your attention to a belief that this one you want and need now exists. Don't concern yourself with the *who* or *how* or *where* or *when*. Concern yourself only with the truth, the truth that this one you now expect is now also expecting you. Have no further faith in disappointment, trust only in the appointment that will draw the two of you together.

BELIEVE . . . CONCEIVE . . . RECEIVE

Remind yourself, "When I believe, I conceive; when I conceive, I receive." Allow this truth to completely dominate your life, abandon yourself to it. Repeatedly affirm it as a fact. "Believe . . . conceive . . . receive."

Reader, whoever you may be, know that you are never alone when you expect your Someone Special. Know that you, too, are Someone Special. This faithful expectation is the first sprightly step toward the union of two Special Ones.

Believe it in spite of everything . . . and you will meet this person in spite of everything.

"THERE IS NO NEED TO BE LONELY"

Let me tell you a charming story that illustrates one way in which you can use this Law of Attraction.

Lucy B. was a woman past fifty, alone and lonely. She courageously faced her situation in two brief observations: "There is no need to be lonely. I will therefore do something about it.

"According to the Bible," she said as she got down to practical business, "there is a greater Power than I Who has promised to supply all my needs. I believe with all my heart that God is able and willing to take an active part in this endeavor. I also believe in my own friendliness, my own capacity to give and receive those necessary elements for a close and satisfying relationship."

She took as her key-to-faith the first part of Matthew 7:7: "Ask, and it shall be given you." She then offered up this affirmative prayer: "I ask for someone who wants and needs those very special qualities which I am prepared to give. I ask for one who is eager to contribute of his own inner riches. I desire a quietness, a gentle understanding, a mutual uniqueness in all our associations. I do not know where or how I shall meet this special person, all I know is that if I ask in faith I shall receive the answer. I therefore ask, claim, rest. The promise is now mine."

"I KNOW YOU EXIST"

She constantly energized her faith during the following days by sending a single, power-packed declaration into the world: "I know you exist." She banished discouraging thoughts and emotions with the truth-decree: "I know you exist."

Sometime later she heard a knock on her door. Upon answering it she was cheerily greeted by an energetic, kindly-looking man of her own age who was selling a line of spices. Always in need of cinnamon and nutmeg for the neighborhood cookies she invited him in. During the course of their conversation they discovered they were both lonely.

He finally left with the twinkling remark, "I'd like to call back in a few days to see how you like my line."

Not exactly dense to his hidden meaning she smilingly asked, "You mean your line of flattery or the spices?"

During the next few weeks it was amazing how much cinnamon she needed and equally amazing how eager he was to supply her need. And one time when she invited him in he invited her out to an evening's entertainment.

They found each other. Two Special Ones became One.

When she was eventually able to tell him of her prayer-plan he laughed, "I've never quite thought of myself as an answer to a woman's prayer, but come to think of it you are also the answer to mine. I needed *some*thing but I didn't know it was some*one*."

WHAT TO DO IF YOU FAIL

I want to speak quite frankly about failure. It is possible that you may need additional ideas for seeing yourself through to a successful conclusion. The following pointers emphasize:

THE ONLY THING YOU HAVE TO DO IS REJECT THE POSSIBILITY OF FAILURE

Believe this. If you can't believe it, assume that you believe it. Proceed as if you did believe it. (Review portions of Chapter

5 where you see yourself as already having attained your desire.)

Above all, never interpret failure *here* as failure *there*. As a matter of fact never think of failure at all because, you see, your Special One may not exist *here*, but he or she certainly exists *there*. When you have faith that the One is *there*, there he will be. If Jack does not find Jill it may be because his Special One is Joan.

Have no faith that anything can thwart you. For nothing can.

REJECT REJECTION, ACCEPT ACCEPTANCE

The above ideas are worth hours, days, weeks of your examination until they are fully planted in your thinking patterns, for they will save you weeks, months, perhaps years of going around with a bewildered, pain-filled heart. So reject all ideas and words of rejection, open yourself only to a full acceptance of things as they truly are, not as they seem to be.

HOW TO BE RIGHT-SIDE-UP

I am intrigued by an unusual procedure which turned a man into an Accepter, which turned his attitudes upside-down and gently deposited him right-side-up for the first time in his life.

He relates, "I was cynical, hostile, loaded with a belief in rejection by everyone and everything. Oh, I put on a shallow show of good manners and all that but I inwardly seethed with the suspicion that others wanted me only for their own selfish convenience. I secretly rejected everyone because I was convinced that everyone secretly rejected me. There was never a more secretly miserable man.

"But my desperation for a free-and-friendly existence shocked me into a desperate self-examination. I bluntly told myself, 'Look, face facts, admit that you are loaded with hostility. Admit that your negativity has brought you nothing but frustration.' With this honest admission I was then able to ask myself, 'Is it possible that you can use this very state of mind as a tool for freeing yourself? Can you turn it to advantage?'

IT IS POSSIBLE FOR YOU!

"The answer was a resounding *yes.* I resolved that from now on I would be *cynical* of *cynicism.* Every time I spoke words of cynicism I would take a sharply cynical attitude toward them. I would look on them with suspicion. I would consider them as enemies of my life-welfare.

"Of course whenever I am doubtful about anything I have the tendency to withdraw, to get away before I get hurt. This is exactly what I did with my bitter speech. I withdrew from it, cut it out, replaced it with a language that spoke of faith and friendliness.

"What happened to me was fantastic and fascinating. I began to see myself in a good way that I had never before known. I actually began to like myself for the first time. My acquaintances also appeared in a new light—as friends. They began to like me in a way that I had never before known."

Thoreau beautifully expresses this idea: "Through our own recovered innocence we discern the innocence of our neighbors."

YOU WILL MAKE A COMFORTING DISCOVERY

If you also have a suspicion that a secret hostility toward people is keeping you at arm's length, I suggest you also take a cynical attitude toward cynicism. Realize that something has been causing you to miss out and this is possibly it. Regardless of how well founded your negativities seem to be, push them out, cut them out, trust in them no longer, speak them no more.

I guarantee you will discover that there are no rude people, only weary people who know no other way to act; that there is no one who can reject you, only someone who painfully rejects himself; that there are no unfriendly people, only nice people who yearn to believe that they are wanted.

Do yourself and your world a favor by showing the way, by using only the "Voice of joy and praise." (Psalm 42:4)

PERTINENT POINTERS FOR YOUR PERSONAL POPULARITY

1. Concentrate on charging the magnet-that-is-you! You will then effortlessly attain an attractive personality.

2. Proceed with the sure knowledge that your own friendliness can make others what you wish them to be.

3. Grasp a full understanding that when you courageously claim what is rightfully yours you are living in the only unselfish and rewarding way.

4. See friends wherever you go!

5. Turn your sensitivities to advantages.

6. Reject all thoughts and feelings of rejection. Accept yourself and know that others also accept you.

7. Know that enriching friendships now exist for you.

8. Have nothing to do with failure . . . and it will have nothing to do with you.

9. Use word power to turn yourself and keep yourself right-side-up!

10. Believe that there are no unfriendly people, only bewildered people who fail to understand how nice they really are.

SAY GOOD-BY TO FEAR, WORRY, AND DISCOURAGEMENT!

Chapter 13

A MAN ONCE TOLD ME, "WHENEVER fear starts chasing me I start running—straight for it!"

I don't believe the secret for conquering fear, timidity, and anxiety can be more magnificently phrased. You might read dozens of books on the conquest of fear and not glean a more dynamic technique than, "Whenever fear starts chasing me I start running—straight for it!"

Smiley Blanton, psychiatrist and physician, phrases the same idea in another way: "Every person suffering from excessive anxiety must first of all accept the fact that the anxiety will disappear only when he faces it on an adult level, a level of reality."[1]

If you will do this, if you will boldly approach that frightening thing, you will make a startling discovery. You will find that the overwhelming majority of fears are nothing more than gigantic bluffs that rob you of your rightful peace of mind.

Now it may be true that you are presently unable to run toward those fearsome things, but I want to show you how you

[1] Norman Vincent Peale and Smiley Blanton, *Faith Is the Answer* (Englewood Cliffs, N. J.: Prentice-Hall, Inc., 1950).

can use your words as winged feet that will speedily and safely carry you over and far beyond those threatening dark valleys of your life.

THE DIFFERENCE BETWEEN RUNNING TOWARD YOUR PROBLEMS AND RUNNING AWAY FROM THEM IS THE DIFFERENCE BETWEEN PEACE OF MIND AND MENTAL CHAOS

No doubt you have heard a troubled soul wearily remark, "If I could just get away from it all I would be happy. If I could just take a trip, move somewhere else, find another job, buy a little home in the country I would be content."

But he wouldn't.

A chief characteristic of the fearful person is the desire to escape, to get away from it all. But it is impossible to get away from it all. *You* are the all . . . and that's all there is.

A man once inherited fifty thousand dollars—but he was in the South Seas to "get away from it all." His nephew got it all. Five years later the puzzled escapist cabled, "What's it all about?" His nephew replied, "Nothing—it's all gone."

Perhaps you are aware that your fears and worries have stranded you in the South Seas where you miss your rightful riches but you don't know how to sail back to your inheritances. This chapter will show you how to do it. You will read of several shipwrecked men and women who left their islands of despair once and for all. But first I want to make an encouraging statement that I think you will remember for a long time.

GET RID OF FEAR AND GOOD THINGS START TO HAPPEN

You see, if fear is now holding you back, a lack of fear will get you on your way. Simple logic. Fear in its many disguises of suspicion, withdrawal, and insecurity pins you down to where you can't do those good things you really want to do. But . . . *get rid of fear and good things start to happen.* Miraculous things. There are spiritual and psychological laws for this which we will discuss later.

HOW TO RID YOURSELF OF ANGRY FEARS

Anger is a skyrocket fueled by fear. We employ anger as a means of denying our feelings of inadequacy (but this cannot succeed, rather we further convince ourselves).

If you want to know what is frightening you (and thus to open your understanding for victory) observe what makes you mad. Some folks have told me it is almost fun to sit back and analyze their emotional explosions. It is something that we should all be willing to do for the sake of our peace, progress, popularity.

Let me tell you how one woman freed herself from distorted self-views which turned into anger. She told me that she was constantly insulted or abused by those whom she met in the course of everyday affairs . . . and that she was pretty mad about it.

"Give me a specific example," I requested.

She scowled. "All right. Last week I went down to the supermarket to cash my check. You know what that heel of a manager said? He curtly shook his head and told me I wasn't well-enough known, but if I cared to establish my credit . . . I exploded. I told him off. I had shopped here for the past three months but this was the end. If I wasn't good enough for him he wasn't good enough for me. I angrily shot out of the door and never went back."

"Why not go back?" I asked.

She threw up her arms and sputtered, "Why, because he insulted my integrity!"

"How could he insult your integrity when it is firmly established?"

She hastily explained, "He hurt my feelings. I knew my check was good. He had no business questioning my honesty."

IF YOU ARE TIRED OF GETTING HURT . . .

"You said you were tired of people hurting you. May I give you some ideas for avoiding so much pain?"

"That's what I want."

"Good. Next pay day go back to that market. For identification, take your driver's license and library card. Tell the manager that you have good credit which you would like him to accept."

She doubtfully shook her head. "That will be embarrassing."

"The way to get rid of painful embarrassment is to see yourself as you really are. Strange, isn't it, that you do not accept the real you, the creditable you? The idea in going back is not to convince the manager of your worth but to convince *yourself*. To discover yourself you must do some exploring. Here is your perfect opportunity for breaking through to a new revelation of your goodness."

She nodded. "I think I see. But it still sounds difficult. I'm not used to facing myself."

"It may be difficult at first but it will also be one of the bravest and most self-enriching things you have ever done. Stand up to these false self-impressions and you will reveal the peaceful qualities you possessed all along."

She went back. She did it. She joyously told me, "It was the break I have wanted for years. I now see how stupid it was for me to defend myself against false self-impressions. When you stoutly accept yourself you see things in a new light." She beamed. "You know what that manager said? He told me he was delighted to know me! He then cashed my check, gave me a market identification card, and personally carried my box of groceries to the car!"

"Continue to break through in all of these everyday matters," I encouraged. "Boldly act in a manner that is opposite to your angers—and they will dissolve in the warmth of your truly loving nature."

DISSOLVE YOUR FEARS BY STOUTLY DENYING THEIR POWER TO BLUFF YOU

If your life is loaded with nagging angers and unreasonable worries you can also apply this "facing and chasing" principle as successfully as did this lady. You will then start drawing all good things to you.

I'd like to give you a specific word-magic technique that will give you astonishing power to banish an overwhelming majority of these false fears. It consists of stoutly standing up to terrifying words and forbidding them to deceive you any longer.

(If you find it difficult to believe that by changing mere *words* you can also change *feelings,* please review earlier chapters which point out the tremendous emotional effect of mere words. Better still, keep reading!)

Take paper and pencil. Write down every word that translates itself into a fear or worry in your life.

Now *deny its power to translate its meaning to you.*

For example:

> **Problem:** "I have no problem—only something that must be—and will be—done."
>
> **Threat:** "I proclaim my freedom from every threat that appears."
>
> **Victim:** "From this day forth I absolutely refuse to think of myself as a victim of circumstance or person."
>
> **Fear:** " 'God hath not given us (me) the spirit of fear; but of power, and of love, and of a sound mind.' " (II Timothy 1:7)
>
> **Luck:** "If this word has any meaning at all, it means I can create my own."
>
> **Rejection:** "I refuse to believe in rejection for I live in a friendly world."
>
> **Trap:** "I deny the power of anyone or anything to make me feel trapped."
>
> **Jinx:** "There is no such word in my vocabulary."
>
> **Misfortune:** "An apparent misfortune is a parent to a new birth of opportunity."
>
> **Worry:** "I've had enough; I reject it altogether."

CALL YOURSELF BY ANOTHER NAME

When you give your words a new identity you also give yourself a bright and overcoming new identity that perfectly matches your new verbal viewpoint.

"I licked fear in my life," said a Tennessee woman, "when I discovered that all fear is really *self*-fear. I never really feared people, I dreaded what they thought of *me*. I wasn't afraid of baffling circumstances, I simply doubted *my* ability to adjust to them. I never shied away from a difficult task, I was shy of *my* capacity to handle it.

"I decided to give myself a new name and live out the meaning of that name. My original middle name was Wanda so I replaced it with a positive word that also started with the letter W. I then called myself Mildred *Winner* Norton. As funny as it sounds, it worked! By associating this single word with my identity I gave myself a new identity—and a winning, optimistic outlook on life."

Several years ago a European businessman was sentenced to prison for a minor crime which struck the headlines because of its unusual nature. He served his time and emerged a free man . . . but not quite. Whenever he applied for a position or settled himself socially his past caught up with him. As unkind and as unjust as it was he could find no place for himself in a society that remembered and punished so persistently.

He changed his name, dressed differently, and settled with his new identity in another city. In short, he freed himself from his hounding past.

Being a brilliant thinker he soon rose to a commanding position in the business world. His daring devices and bold plans again brought his name into the newspapers. But this time it was a different story; he was hailed as the genius that he was.

All because he gave himself a new identity, cut off those past associations, gave himself a fresh start.

His story had a happy climax, for when he later disclosed his true identity he was freely accepted. Who could justly condemn such a valorous individual who had proved his social worth?

I mention this incident to once more show you the imperative need for seeing yourself as that new personality, for freeing yourself from *all* those fearful and life-strangling concepts of yourself.

DON'T SENTENCE YOURSELF TO LIFE-IMPRISONMENT

Do you feel imprisoned by anxiety and apprehension? If so, it is probable that you also speak sentences that are full of anxiety and apprehension . . . and you thus sentence yourself to life-imprisonment.

Mrs. Julia T. was just such an individual. Her particular life-sentences consisted in scolding her adolescent son whenever he arrived home a few minutes late or whenever he expressed a desire to stay overnight with chums. Her fear that he would "go wild" expressed itself in anger—which, of course, aroused a rebellion in her son to have his own way, regardless of her explosive cautions.

It was pointed out to her that her anxious speech could be a principal factor in actually driving the young man into a wild state. She was further made to understand that quiet, reasonable, beyond-her-own-fears speech was the only type that would enable him to grasp the values of her advice.

She caught herself just in time by applying word magic. She asked him if he had a good time, she suggested that they check with the parents of the overnight chums, she used loving words to give him the feeling of being trusted. She was delighted at his cooperative response. Wrathful scenes turned into peaceful mother-and-son discussions. Because she freed herself from life-imprisoning sentences she also freed her son!

Like Mrs. T., a complete pardon is yours for the asking! If you will faithfully apply your word-power techniques you will be free, you will joyously be surprised at all the ways and means you find for doing this or that. You will see that you had unused powers within you all the time.

RESOLVE TO BE RESOLUTE

Resolve that every time a fear-word strikes you you will strike back with an exhilarating cry of faith in God and in yourself. Put your weight on what you *should* say—and what you *shouldn't* say will have no weight on you at all!

GIVE FEAR A COLD SHOULDER AND IT WILL LEAVE YOU WITH A WARM FEELING

Deny every fear or worry the right to bother you! Get indignant! Refuse! Reject! Shout no! Shout it out and get it out! Contradict! Refuse to recognize! Make fear a stranger! Give fear a cold shoulder and it will leave you with a warm feeling.

Here is one place where negative speech (saying no!) will bring about positive results!

By doing this you will develop X-ray vision, you will gain a new awareness that quietly changes every threatening thing into a challenge or an opportunity or a new beginning or a fresh blessing. You will wonder what in the world was frightening you all the time.

A San Francisco mechanic who found a glorious release from anxiety asked the question, "It works, but I don't know why. Can you tell me?"

"It's very simple," he was told. "Every word has a certain meaning to you; therefore you must emotionally react according to your interpretation of the word. Change its meaning and you change your feeling toward life. When you no longer believe in fear you are no longer able to fear."

A young man of considerable ability who was employed as a shipping clerk for a paint manufacturing company was unexpectedly offered an advancement to shipping foreman. He found himself tied in emotional knots for he feared he could not live up to the new responsibilities. The very word *promotion* was a terror to him.

But he wanted the promotion more than he wanted his fears, so the first thing he did was to *interpret promotion as a good thing*. Now what do you do with a good thing? You go after it. So as a second step he studied the job's requirements by asking questions and by observing the present foreman. His third step was to step boldly into place; he took charge of the job. The rest was routine. In time, this new good thing was just as casually handled as his old job. By *interpreting* additional responsibility as good, he gave himself additional powers to *make* it good in a practical way.

YOUR WORDS ARE ROAD SIGNS . . . AND YOU DRIVE THROUGH LIFE ACCORDING TO YOUR INTERPRETATION

Remember that your words are your road signs. They are not the roads themselves, they are merely signs that cause you to act according to what you believe they mean.

PUT UP SOME NEW SIGNS!

You have probably driven your car down the highway only to slow down at signs that read: DANGEROUS . . . ROAD CLOSED . . . SLIPPERY . . . BRIDGE OUT. You wisely observed these warnings for they pointed out very real highway conditions.

But life is not a closed road . . . only if you have erected your own fearful signs and read them as real dangers . . . only if you believe them.

So picture yourself as comfortably speeding along the highway of life. See some new signs that read: OPEN ROAD . . . FREELY PROCEED . . . HAPPINESS AHEAD.

Put full confidence in your new road signs and you will freely enjoy the pleasurable conditions.

PSYCHOLOGY POINTS OUT . . .

Professor William James of Harvard pointed out that physical movement can be used as a tool in liberating the self from timidity and terror. For example, a child who shirks from dogs is first given cardboard dogs as playthings; as his confidence grows he is gradually brought into association with real dogs. An attorney who had an unreasonable fear of water (caused by a childhood spill in a river) forced himself to spend several hours a week at a nearby lake. Before long you could hardly tell him from a fish!

(Incidentally, perhaps you now better understand some of the techniques in this book that stress physical action as well as verbal declarations.)

I now want to specifically show you how to employ your joint tools of physical movement and word power to gain that blessed state of 24-hour liberation of mind and spirit.

WALK AND TALK YOUR WAY TO EMOTIONAL GLADNESS

A man whom we will call Walter developed a unique and workable plan for freeing himself from false feelings of uneasiness. Whenever he felt depressed and hemmed in he closed all the doors of his home and stood in a room where it would be necessary for him to open several doors in order to arrive at the freedom of the outside air.

As he stood in the center of the house he dropped all thought of his problem and concentrated on feelings of emotional freedom. He then walked out—casually opening the doors before him—while declaring, "I am walking toward freedom concerning this matter. The way is opening before me. There is absolutely nothing in my way. I am free!"

He summoned all the emotional intensity possible by thinking of freedom, speaking of freedom, and walking toward freedom. He refused to dwell on the problem itself; his only object was an emotional release from his jittery state.

"FREE . . . FREE . . . FREE!"

As he stepped outside into the broad expanse of the entire world he looked skyward, took a deep breath and joyously exclaimed, "I am free . . . free . . . free!"

This simple exercise of impressing himself with freedom gradually released those subconscious feelings of anxiety which had no logical support in the first place.

So impressed was Walter with the impression he had made on himself that he decided to carry it a step further . . . and I invite you to also try it.

He printed the single letter L (for *Liberty*) just above the doorknob (making it just heavy enough for him to see but not so conspicuous that it attracted curious questions). This constant reminder gave him additional power to feel liberty on the inside as well as seeing it on the outside. By proclaiming his liberty as he stepped through the doorway he induced that emotional surge that more and more made life-liberty a bright and living experience.

PUT YOUR EMOTIONS TO WORK FOR YOU

If you will also practice this "freedom march" you will find it helpful, logical, practical, whatever your timidity might be. Let's make it clear as to how and why it works:

1. You feel yourself to be in the center of apprehension (as you stand in the center of the house).
2. All solutions (the closed doors of the hours) seem closed.
3. By taking physical and verbal steps toward freedom (by opening the doors and freely marching through while speaking your affirmations) you charge yourself with a new feeling—that of release.
4. By your stepping outside and boldly declaring yourself to be free your emotions have no choice but to follow your leading —and you *are* free.

As soon as you take command of yourself, as soon as you successfully impress yourself with the idea of freedom, you will be actually free of those clinging distresses. Your emotions will then pull with you instead of against you. You will then be at liberty to think clearly and solve your problem in whatever way seems best . . . or it is possible you may find it wasn't really worth bothering about.

A salesman who delivered bakery goods to groceries and restaurants was requested by his firm to add at least one new customer per week to his route. Because he felt that he wasn't a "natural born salesman" (whatever that is) he wondered how long his job would last.

Help came from his route foreman who rode alongside one day: "When you walk up to a prospective customer just pretend that he is *already* on your route. Talk to him in the same easy, self-confident manner in which you speak to your established customers. See no stranger, see someone you've chatted with a hundred times. *Hi! What's up? Look what I've got!* Something like that. Not brash, of course, just as one friendly soul to another. This kind of talk breaks down your inhibitions concerning your abilities. As your naturalness grows, so will your sales-appeal. You may find yourself with more customers than you can handle."

When he put his free speech to work, it worked for him. Freedom became a practical reality . . . as did a bigger paycheck.

HAVE NO DOUBTS . . . YOU WILL PERFORM MUCH BETTER

You might find it fun to devise your own workable methods for attaining a consciousness of freedom. How about declaring yourself at complete liberty from emotional darkness as you enter a lighted room? Or you might accept the beginning of each day as a single forward step toward the illumination of your inner self.

You are invited to persistently practice, regardless of how you presently feel. You see, the whole idea is to change those hampering feelings that resist change. Make no mistake, any entrenched habit will try to hang on. But hang on yourself and take counsel from wise Sophocles: "One must learn by doing the thing; for though you think you know it you have no certainty until you try."

It is probable that you will not achieve 100 per cent effectiveness the first few times you try, but if you feel even 5 per cent better you have solid ground for knowing that you can also feel 50 per cent and 80 per cent and eventually 100 per cent better.

Take this as your daily, prayerful declaration of independence: "I will walk at liberty." (Psalm 119:45)

"INSPECT YOUR RICHES IN ABUNDANCE"

Before beginning his Sunday morning message, a minister asked his congregation to do an unusual thing. He invited them outside with the remark, "Come with me to inspect your riches in abundance."

As they stood outside he gestured toward the mountains and exclaimed, "Over here you see God's power to create mighty mountains and lush valleys for you."

He gestured in another direction. "And over here you observe God's provision of farms and orchards."

He flung an arm skyward and said, "Up there you see God's benevolence in providing you with warmth and sunshine."

He gestured downward toward the city and continued, "Down there you see God's tender care in supplying friends who have an abundance of love and kindness toward you."

The pastor then gave a sweeping gesture with both arms and concluded, "Wherever you look you see an abundance of all you want and need, all for which you yearn, all for which you hope, all for which you pray."

He then led them inside the church where he proceeded to preach a sermon entitled, "How to Rid Yourself of Fear."

His congregation was at first baffled at the apparent contradiction between his open-air remarks and his sermon topic. The themes of abundance and fear seemed incompatible. But they began to see the light as he proceeded: "Fear has its roots in a belief in limitation . . . it is impossible to be anxious when you know all your wants are provided for . . . greed and envy are but outer symptoms of inner disbelief . . . a simple trust in all the goodness of God brings all the goodness of God to the one who trusts."

As the pastor bade them farewell at the door an old saint grasped his hand and wept, "I have been wrong for sixty years. All my life I have quoted the first verse of the Twenty-Third Psalm but until this morning I never knew the practical interpretation of, 'The Lord is my shepherd; I shall not want.' "

CONSENT TO ABUNDANCE . . . AND YOU WILL HAVE IT

It is possible that you, too, have been wrong. If so, I urge you to stop believing in limitation, stop talking it, stop thinking it, stop acting it, stop listening to it, stop consenting to it . . . and start believing, talking, thinking, acting, listening, and consenting to full abundance for *you . . . yourself . . . personally.*

And then you will be right.

And then you won't be afraid of anything.

No millionaire worries as to where his next dollar is coming from.

You are a millionaire, for the Book says, "The earth is full of thy riches."

Therefore you need never worry about anything.

God says so.

Now you say so.

And then you won't be afraid of anything.

"I BELIEVE!"

The first suggestion I want to give you for drawing abundance into your life consists in writing out and claiming a Divine promise every day. Take a sheet of paper and copy down the listed verses as follows:

SUNDAY

"The earth is full of thy (my) riches." (Psalm 104:24)

MONDAY

"I rejoiced because my wealth was great." (Job 31:25)

TUESDAY

"Abundance of peace so long as the moon endureth." (Psalm 72:7)

WEDNESDAY

"My God shall supply all your (my) need." (Philippians 4:19)

THURSDAY

"Whatsoever he (I) doeth shall prosper." (Psalm 1:3)

FRIDAY

"The world is mine, and the fulness thereof." (Psalm 50:12)

SATURDAY

"Moreover the profit of the earth is for all." (Ecclesiastes 5:9)

Early each morning read and meditate your affirmations. Now take a bright crayon and print over the verse large letters that affirm, I BELIEVE! Carry this attitude of mind with you throughout the day, make it your heartfelt belief, accept it as being true of yourself. No matter how you *feel,* accept it as entirely true.

At the end of your weekly period once more read and verbally declare your acceptance. Now consider it as done. Consider God's promises as fulfilled in your life. Be anxious no longer, only grateful, for a grateful heart implies the thing as being done, the gift as received. When you arrive at this inner state of grateful acceptance it *will* be done, you will outwardly have that which you first inwardly accepted.

AFFIRM YOUR DAILY INCREASE

As a second technique, try what I call the "Monthly Increase" method. Look at your calendar. If it happens to be the tenth day of the month affirm that at least ten good things will come your way during the day. The following day declare that you have increased the abundance of your blessings to eleven. Continue to add to your blessings for each day of the month. On the last day proclaim complete abundance of every desirable thing in your life. Now start another cycle of increasing abundance with the new month.

The time will come when you will be in the position of the successful song-writer who was asked, "Aren't you afraid of running out of good ideas?"

"I've no time to be afraid of running out," he replied, "I'm too busy running into!"

THERE IS PLENTY OF LIFE TO GO AROUND

A prominent Atlantic Coast restaurateur, who dwells in a full abundance of material and spiritual wealth, has his own special formula for cheering up his worried diners. Over the years his patrons have recognized something triumphantly different about his whole manner of living. His easy-going friendliness has a way of opening up those repressed worries so that they tell him all. And then *he* tells *them*. He states:

"I'm no psychologist but do you know what I find underneath all this fright and flight in folks who come into my restaurant? A plain old worry that there just isn't enough life to go around! They accept the fact that there's plenty of food in my kitchens to supply their physical needs but when it comes to those spiritual nourishments of tranquillity and enthusiasm they think life's restaurant has gone out of business.

"You know what I tell them? I tell them they are being ridiculous! Far from getting insulted they eagerly listen to every word I say, for deep in their hearts they *want* to believe in abundance but they're just too smothered by dark fears to see the light.

"I ask them to look over the menu and order what they want. Like a T-bone steak? Order it. Prefer lobster thermidor? Order it. How about some coffee? Order it. Do you have a taste for cherry pie? Order it. Like chocolate cake? Order it.

"MAKE IT A DAILY PRACTICE"

"As soon as they are served with the dishes they desire I pull up a chair, order a cup of coffee for myself, and we start chatting. I ask them to think of the world as a huge restaurant which will supply every good thing they request. I ask them to look at the menu and see the bountiful dishes freely offered—joy, satisfaction, restfulness, affection, even material wealth. I then tell them to make it a daily practice to walk up to life and order what they want. I make it clear that there are certain Divine Laws that will wait on them just as surely as did my waiters. But just as they entered my restaurant in full confidence that they will be served whatever they desire they must also enter into life with the same confidence that these Spiritual Laws will also bountifully wait on them.

"I make it a practice to carefully observe the faces of my friends as I finish my little table-talk. Some shake their heads in polite disbelief; others nod in hopeful acceptance. And do you know something? It's the nodders who always come back to tell me that they are beginning to royally feast on wonderful foods they have never tasted before!"

ORDER IT!

If you, too, will become a nodder to the Spiritual Laws of Plenty, you will never shake in fear again.

Believe that what you want is on the menu . . . and order it!

Would you like a deep tranquillity in the very roots of your being?

Order it!

Do you desire greater material abundance?

Order it!

Do you want someone to love you?

Order it!

You will feast royally every day, for "No good thing will he withhold." (Psalm 84:11)

TEN GOOD IDEAS FOR YOUR DAILY PRACTICE

1. Whenever fear starts chasing you, start running—straight for it.

2. Get rid of fear, and good things start to happen!

3. Unmask those unreasonable and groundless fears.

4. Deny the power of anxiety over you; affirm confidence in its place.

5. Don't sentence yourself to life-imprisonment by speaking binding (negative) sentences.

6. Give fear a cold shoulder and it will always leave you with a warm feeling.

7. Drive through life with optimistic, hopeful road signs.

8. Inwardly accept your life-abundances and you will outwardly experience them.

9. Consistently practice your techniques for abundance.

10. Order what you want—and expect to be served!

PEACE OF MIND THROUGH WORD POWER

Chapter 14

LET ME TELL YOU A STORY THAT WILL show you how you can use your word power for inducing peaceful, restful feelings.

I know an Arizona rancher who used to have the absolute maximum of self-punishing speech habits. No incident was too trifling for him to turn it into a nerve-wracking experience with his hostile, bitter language. You can correctly guess that he was as jittery as he was angrily talkative.

One evening, during a quiet moment in the patio, I urged him to start blessing himself with words of blessing, but he bluntly replied, "This psychology business may be all right for you, but I'm the rugged, outdoor type. It's always been rough and tumble for me, so why shouldn't I talk that way?" He gave a weary shrug that indicated his hopelessness and added, "Nothing can be done about it anyway."

"What if I told you that you destroy your peace of mind every time you speak destructively?"

"You may be right," he admitted, "but I can't have everything. Of course I want a peaceful mind, but . . ."

Realizing he wanted help but was too proud and cynical to listen to detailed suggestions, I ventured a different course. "All right, forget the psychology. Instead, let's play a game which has but a single rule."

He loosened himself enough to reply, "Okay, I'll play along."

"Here's what to do," I said. "Several times a day, whenever

you speak to yourself or to others, just imagine that you are standing on the edge of the Grand Canyon. By the way, you have actually stood there many times haven't you?"

"Of course. But what's that got to do with anything?"

"Imagine yourself standing there whenever you speak," I repeated. "Now the Grand Canyon would probably echo anything you shout, wouldn't it?"

"Perfect reproduction in some places," he agreed.

YOUR WORDS WILL FAITHFULLY ECHO BACK TO YOU

"All right. As you imaginatively stand there and shout, just imagine that everything that you say comes right back to you in perfect reproduction; that is, you will actually feel an emotion that perfectly matches the meanings of your words. For example, if you shout *confusion* you will actually *feel* confusion; if you shout *peace* you will fill yourself with peaceful emotions."

"Sounds easy enough," he admitted.

"So start speaking only that which you want to return to you in the form of emotions. Echo peaceful emotions back to yourself with peaceful words. If you will practice this echo-technique you will sooner or later feel profound changes within yourself. You will be calm and peaceful, you will rest comfortably in all those trifling incidents that now upset you. Is it worth a try?"

"Okay, but don't tell anyone I fell for your line," he agreed with a good-natured grin.

I had to leave shortly afterward but I was interested in discovering what his few hours of practice had done for him. "How are the echoes?" I inquired.

"You tricked me," he accused with a friendly smile. "You know very well how I'm doing. Just as you predicted, I already have a glimmer of something good going on inside. Yesterday in town I dropped into a shop to pick up a saddle which I had left for repair a couple of weeks ago. When he told me it wasn't ready as yet I felt like bawling him out—but I remembered the echoes and so I told him okay, I know you're busy, see you next week. My patient words made me feel great! Then on the drive home I got angry with myself for forgetting to pay a bill while in town—you see, I like to think of myself as highly efficient. I echoed some reassuring words by telling myself that it really makes no difference, the bill will get paid. This calm inner speech helped me to see that I was confusing efficiency with nervousness. What a relief *this* gave me! I can see even greater things ahead."

SPEAK "GOOD WORDS AND COMFORTABLE WORDS" AND YOU WILL ECHO GOOD AND COMFORTABLE FEELINGS

If you, like the rancher, think nothing can be done about it, I urge you to get the habit of drawing peaceful emotions to yourself by speaking "Good words and comfortable words." (Zechariah 1:13) Dwell in a verbal atmosphere of peace and harmony. Carry it with you wherever you go and you will sweeten the air of every surrounding circumstance.

This is one of those entirely possible things which will prove itself to you a dozen times a day.

DIRECT YOUR ATTENTION TOWARD TRANQUILLITY

The bee directs his attention toward the sweet blossom . . . and carries away a full supply of honey.

The ship turns her prow toward the restful harbor . . . and lightly rests in its calm waters.

If you will simply direct your attention toward the tranquil state, you will experience the tranquil state. You will become that which you contemplate becoming. I have a friend who is an exciting expert on the subject of astronomy. He can do almost anything with it, from naming the stars to building his own telescopes. Why? Because he gives it every spare moment of his attention. By directing his mind toward his chosen goal he achieves daily success with it.

Peace of mind is largely a matter of attention. And attention is always a matter of choice. You can direct yourself in any direction you like.

Moreover, peace of mind is largely a matter of verbal attention. Every word you utter is a signal that flashes either a *Welcome* or a *Keep Out* to the Kingdom of Peace. You are always signalling to yourself in one way or the other. Every time you speak a certain way you are directing your attention toward that certain way.

Peaceful folks have arrived at the blissful state where their attention is constantly fixed on the blissful.

Perhaps the utter simplicity of this truth is the only reason why you have not attained peace of mind as a reality in your life.

But simple truths can be realized by applying simple methods. And then your life will not be complicated any more.

MAKE PEACE OF MIND YOUR HOBBY

I heard of a man who made a hobby—yes, a hobby and a richly rewarding one—of turning his attention to peace within himself and in the world without. (He discovered that peace was catching—every time he impressed it upon himself it also magically impressed itself upon his daily contacts with his outside world.)

He set himself to the recreational task of devising all sorts of ways and means for inducing restful emotions, four of which are listed below for your personal use.

1. Read, memorize, and absorb literary passages that convey ideas of harmony, unity, gentleness. This could include Scripture, sayings of noble men and women of history, poetry, philosophical precepts, proverbs, and so on.
2. Listen to and lose yourself in peaceful music. This does not mean you must omit music of a more exciting nature, but rather eliminate the harsh, the mournful, the nerve-wracking. (Incidentally, entire books have been written on the overpowering effect of music upon emotional states. What happens to your heart when you hear a favorite, dreamy love-song?)

3. Build a scrapbook of pictures and photographs that suggest and harmonize with the peaceful life . . . a lovely lake, a sleeping child, a country chapel, a blossoming meadow. Print suitable titles beneath each, such as *Repose, Silence.* Whenever you feel disturbed, meditate upon your peaceful scenes, imagine yourself as actually within them, sharing their tranquillity. Take yourself away from your old feelings until you absorb the restful feelings, which will surely permeate you.

4. "Seek peace, and pursue it." (Psalm 34:14)

PEACE IS A MIRROR

It will be impossible for you to pay rapt attention to peace and not be affected by it. Peace is like a mirror; it will perfectly reflect whatever you set before it.

If you will consistently concentrate your attentions on the lovely you will be lovely.

BAKE A SAY-CAKE!

A Colorado homemaker explains her unusual and amusing method for directing her daily thoughts and energies toward the joyous:

"Every day-break I bake a say-cake. My say-cake is loaded with all sorts of sweet verbal ingredients—a cupful of cheery remarks, a generous amount of enthusiasm, a full quart of prayer, a pint of humor. I top it off with the sweet frosting of acceptance of every peaceful thing in the world!

"It fully satisfies my inner hunger all day long. Not only that but just about everyone wants to know my secret recipe!"

Bake a say-cake every day-break. It satisfies!

"WHY NOT RELAX NOW?"

All of us have the tendency to forget rather easily, even when concerned with such a vital matter as mental and physical relaxation. A Seattle businessman, concerned with increased tension and irritability among his employees, pinned three metal buttons on his coat, each with a question mark printed on it. He naturally aroused considerable curiosity as he mingled with his employees. A secretary who could stand the suspense no longer finally asked him what they meant.

"The first asks—*are you relaxed?*"

"What about the second?"

"If not, why not?"

"And the third?"

He tapped the third button. "That's the most important question of all. It asks—*why not relax now?*"

His appeal to curiosity led to a wholesale practice of relaxation, which in turn led to a happier and more efficient staff.

Surprise yourself throughout the day by asking yourself these three questions . . . and answer yourself with a positive declaration and practice of present relaxation.

LOOK FOR THE SUNNY SIDE . . . AND SEE IT!

I was talking with a friend about the power of speech to mold healthy emotional habits when I dropped the remark, "Make every adverb a glad-verb and you'll be glad you did."

"Oh, oh . . ." he replied as he cut the air with a sharp gesture, "here we go again . . . that old stuff about looking on the bright side. Well, let me tell you that I've tried it, but every time I try to see the sunny side someone comes along to darken everything."

"Hold everything, Paul," I requested, "especially your judgment."

When he agreed to suspend himself for the moment I continued. "Tell me, what do you expect life to bring your way in the next few days? What do you honestly expect?"

"Nothing very good," he admitted, "I expect almost anything miserable to happen."

"*Why* do you expect all these bad things?"

He hopelessly threw up his arms. "They've happened in the past. Isn't that reason enough to expect them in the future?"

"No it isn't, not in the least. Tell me, since you look for unfavorable occurrences, exactly who is going to cause them to happen?"

He shrugged. "I haven't the slightest idea."

"Will a loving God be the cause?"

"Of course not."

"Will your friends?"

"No."

"Do you have enemies who will go out of their way to cause you unhappiness?"

"No."

"Then exactly who is behind all these miserable expectations?"

After a moment of thought he replied, "Maybe I'm afraid of *circumstances.*"

"But that doesn't make sense. You know that you create your own circumstances; they can't create themselves."

"I suppose," he reluctantly agreed.

"Will you also then concede that your present pessimistic outlook has a lot to do with your depressing circumstances?"

DON'T BE YOUR OWN WORST ENEMY!

"I think," he grinned, "that you're saying I'm my own worst enemy."

I returned the grin. "I think you're right. Your humility is refreshing. I want you to do something for me, or rather for yourself. Will you change your expectations from this moment on to expectations of pleasurable conditions?

"All right."

SEE WHAT YOU **WANT** TO SEE

"For a change, see only what you want to see. Resolve to greet the world in the way you would like the world to greet you—with bounce and blessing."

"I'll try. Where do I begin?"

"Look out the window. What do you see?"

"People."

"No, you see *nice* people. Folks with whom you can share pleasant experiences. Look at your hands. What do you see?"

"Hands."

"Strong, capable hands that will successfully complete any task you undertake."

As soon as he got the idea I gave him several techniques for self-mastery through speech-mastery. A few weeks and a few chats later he exclaimed, "Mr. Howard, I'm amazed! As I practiced the sunny response *before* something happened, it also happened *afterward*. The whole thing seems backward, but it works like true magic! Take yesterday. Down at the office is a certain sour-tongued district manager who rarely has anything nice for anyone. I told myself that henceforth I would see him as a fine—though perhaps emotionally mixed up—fellow. So I gave everything I had to this nice man—a smile, a compliment, told him a funny joke. How he melted! He *is* a fine fellow!"

IT IS UP TO YOU . . . SO LIFT YOURSELF UP!

It *seems* backward, but it isn't. We cause—by our expectations, attitudes, words, thoughts—things to happen. The exact nature of these things—whether grief or gladness—is up to us.

HOW TO CHANGE YOUR EXPECTATIONS—AND YOUR LIFE—TO THE SATISFYING

Would you like to train your viewpoints and attitudes so that they automatically create bright experiences? Here is a worthwhile experiment that will show you how:

1. Somewhere in your home you have a clock. For the purpose of the experiment, imagine that the clock (perhaps like your life) is in a dark, unsatisfactory corner.
2. Turn and look at it. You will see exactly what you expect to see—the clock ticking away its life in the dark corner.
3. Move the clock to another location in the room; a sunnier, cheerier place.
4. As you go through the day and wish to check the time,

expect to see the clock in its new and better location. This may be difficult at first for over the months you have trained your expectancies toward seeing it in the old place . . . and that is what you *will* see. Even when you don't want to look in the dark corner you are compelled to do so by your habit-system.

5. Continue to direct your glance toward the cheery location, expect to see the clock in its new light. Say to yourself, "In order to enjoy the satisfaction of having the correct time I must train myself to expect the new, the sunny." And after a while you will have the happy habit of looking only for the new and sunny. And at last you will truly see what you really want to see!

PEACE OF MIND **DOES** EXIST FOR YOU!

How do you apply the experiment to your life? By constantly directing yourself toward the new, the refreshing, the cheery, the peaceful. *Peace of mind exists for you just as surely as the clock exists.* Your part is to steadily look until you see.

The kind of words you speak correspond to the locations—either cheery or dismal—at which you direct your glance. You might say that as you *speak* you *peek.*

See what you want to see and you'll be what you want to be!

The story is told of one of the Duke of Wellington's generals during the first hours of the Battle of Waterloo.

"General," asked an aide, "what is the first thing you expect?"

"To defeat Napoleon," the officer replied.

"The *first* thing you expect?" gasped the aide.

"How would you have it?" asked the general, "the *last* thing I expect?"

"I'D GIVE ALMOST ANYTHING . . ."

A lonely and depressed woman once came to her doctor with the pathetic plea, "Doctor, what do I need to give me peace of mind? Money is of no interest to me, I care little for the latest fashions. What do I want from life? What is this thing I crave so desperately that I'd give almost anything to attain it?"

The doctor, who had studied the lady for several months, instantly replied, "You simply need to be convinced that you are all right."

She tilted her head in an inquiring fashion. "To be convinced that I am all right? As simple as that?"

"As a perfectly normal human being you need certain basic supplies in order to enjoy a tranquil spirit. Probably the most important of these is the need for feeling all right, for being accepted, for knowing that someone cares for you."

She thoughtfully nodded. "Someone to tell me that I am all right, that I'm doing fine. Yes, that would be just wonderful. But," she hopelessly shrugged. "I'm all alone in the world."

"That is not quite accurate, but we'll skip it for now. As a matter of fact, you *are* all right—at this very instant."

Her face hopefully brightened. "I *am?*"

"Yes, of course you are. But I must frankly tell you that I can never convince you of it. Neither can anyone else."

Her expression drooped, she muttered almost bitterly, "For a moment I thought you could help me."

"Mrs. Walker," the doctor said, "suppose I tried to convince you that the world is flat. Could I suceed?"

"No."

"Why not?"

She gestured vaguely. "Because it's contrary to what I believe."

"Exactly. And that's why I can never give you the peace of mind you require. You can only accept what you believe . . . and you believe yourself to be a lonely failure."

"So what do we do?" she humbly asked.

GO INTO BUSINESS FOR YOURSELF

"It's what *you* do. I can only give you a temporary lift that will vanish the moment you leave here. I happen to know that you are fundamentally all right but you must believe it for yourself before it does you any good. I want you to go into business for yourself. Actually, the only thing you need is a change of mind about yourself."

"How do I make the change?"

The doctor rose. "Come back this afternoon. I will give you a secret little speech which I want you to deliver to yourself twenty times a day. I have no doubts that you will start changing your mind—and your entire mental atmosphere from depression to peace."

When she returned he gave her a specially prepared affirmation which she read aloud:

> **"I am all right!**
> No matter what I think of myself, **I am all right.**
> Regardless of others, **I am all right.**
> In spite of past experiences, **I am all right.**
> When things appear all wrong, **I am all right.**
> When things appear all right, **I am all right.**
> Wherever I am, **I am all right.**
> Whatever I am, **I am all right.**
> **I am all right!"**

The woman stared in puzzlement at the paper. "But how can I honestly declare that I am all right when I am all wrong?"

"I know it seems strange," he told her, "but the whole idea is to uncover your real, worthy, affable self of which you are not presently aware. Separate yourself from every word or thought that implies that you are all wrong and associate with words and thoughts that tell you the truth about yourself—that you are acceptable, that you are fundamentally all right. I observe that you are a very sensitive person; sensitive people are wide open to both false and true appraisals. Open up this sensitivity of yours to the truth for a change. Don't question it, simply talk yourself into believing it. You will find you were telling the truth all along!"

DISCOVER THE WONDERFUL TRUTH ABOUT YOURSELF!

When the doctor later inquired as to her progress she smilingly summed up her vastly improved mental outlook (and more than improved social circumstances) with a convincing, "I am all right!"

And so are you!

You will experimentally know that you are all right when you say it long enough and strong enough.

The Bible commands: "Let the weak say, I am strong." (Joel 3:10)

Great heavens, it was right in front of us all along!

HOW TO RELEASE YOURSELF FROM DAILY TENSION

A colonel of the United States Army, tense and jittery from weeks of intense duty, dragged himself to the post chapel where he wearily lowered himself into a chair. "Chaplain," he said, "I'll come right to the point. How do I get rid of nerves? Is it really possible to live a quiet inner life amidst so much external confusion?"

The chaplain nodded. "I assure you that you can leave this chapel with a technique that will give you everyday restfulness."

The colonel drew a deep breath, slowly exhaled a sigh of relief, and asked, "How do I do it?"

The chaplain smiled. "You just did."

"What?"

"That deep sigh you just took. It is probably the only relief-giving emotion you have expressed today. It made you feel good, didn't it?"

"Why, yes. Your encouraging words made me feel so good I couldn't help but feel relieved."

The chaplain pointed out, "Your *own* words can have an equally soothing effect. In fact, as you grasp the idea, much more."

The chaplain then supplied him with the following suggestions which you, too, can use for inducing emotional quietness.

SIGH IT . . . SAY IT . . . FEEL IT

1. Start the morning with the quiet assumption that this will be one of the most delightful days you have ever had, regard-

less of your forthcoming affairs. Pretend that it is bedtime of the same evening and imaginatively see yourself as stretching in complete content at the restful day you have just enjoyed. Quietly sigh, "What a wonderful day!" Now come back to the present.

2. From time to time, throughout the day, deliberately inhale a deep breath of fresh, clean air and slowly exhale while picturing any tensions as vanishing into the air with your breath. Sigh, "Peace . . . peace . . . peace."

3. At every opportunity relax at least one part of your body, perhaps your jaw, your arms, your hands. Reinforce this relaxation by sighing, "I am relaxed . . . relaxed . . . it is done . . . I am relaxed . . . it is done."

4. At bedtime, repeat the very same affirmation you declared in the morning. *Do it even if the day didn't turn out 100 per cent perfect; for, you see, it really was a wonderful day; it was simply that you didn't happen to absorb all of your surrounding quietness.* Your day might be likened to a seed. It is *always* a good day for a seed, even though it has not as yet stretched forth into the fullness of the free air and warming sunshine. But even better days are coming.

5. Continue in this until your feelings match your words. Then you will be more than a match for anything!

You will be encouraged to practice this technique if you understand why it works so well. A simple explanation is that you convince your receptive subconscious mind with the idea of relaxation . . . and the obedient subconscious has no choice but to turn it into an actual experience. The whole idea is to call the bluff on those surface feelings which imply that nervousness is your only fate and state.

KNOW THIS!

If you are capable of being nervous, you are also capable of being peaceful. If shakiness is a constant state, quietness can also be a constant state. You now know this as an intellectual truth; before long you will know it as a marvelous emotional experience. You will know what William Hazlitt meant by, "The only true retirement is that of the heart."

EXHAUST ALL YOUR POSSIBILITIES FOR PEACE

If you feel you have exhausted all possibilities for attaining a serene spirit, I now invite you to turn around and start exhausting every word and thought that contradicts this false impression.

Remember that a peaceful belief will lead to a peaceful relief that will abide always.

"Peace be unto you." (Luke 24:36)

APPLY THESE PEACEFUL TECHNIQUES FOR PEACEFUL LIVING

1. Practice speaking only "Good words and comfortable words."

2. Constantly direct your interest and attention toward the restful, the quiet.

3. Make peace of mind your leisurely—but determined—hobby.

4. Bake a say-cake every day-break!

5. Surprise yourself several times a day by asking, "Why not relax?" Answer yourself by applying one or more of the peace-plans supplied in the chapter.

6. Talk about good things, think about good things, look for good things, expect good things—and accept them as natural gifts.

7. Know that mental tranquillity is a personal actuality. Continue to look until you see it as a personal experience.

8. Quietly inform yourself that you are fundamentally all right . . . for you are only speaking the truth!

9. Observe, "Let the weak say, I am strong," and you will observe a new strength.

10. Claim and believe that every day is a wonderful day.

INDEX

C

D

E

M

N

O

P

M